Digital Health and Patient Data

Patients with unmet needs will continue to increase as no viable nor adequate treatment exists. Meanwhile, healthcare systems are struggling to cope with the rise of patients with chronic diseases, the ageing population and the increasing cost of drugs.

What if there is a faster and less expensive way to provide better care for patients using the right digital solutions and transforming the growing volumes of health data into insights? The increase of digital health has grown exponentially in the last few years. Why is there a slow uptake of these new digital solutions in the healthcare and pharmaceutical industries? One of the key reasons is that patients are often left out of the innovation process. Their data are used without their knowledge, solutions designed for them are developed without their input and healthcare professionals refuse their expertise. This book explores what it means to empower patients in a digital world and how this empowerment will bridge the gap between science, technology and patients. All these components need to co-exist to bring value not only to the patients themselves but to improve the healthcare ecosystem.

Patients have taken matters into their own hands. Some are equipped with the latest wearables and applications, engaged in improving their health using data, empowered to make informed decisions and ultimately are experts in their disease(s). They are the e-patients. The other side of the spectrum are patients with minimal digital literacy but equally willing to donate their data for the purpose of research. Finding the right balance when using digital health solutions becomes as critical as the need to develop a disease-specific solution.

For the first time, the authors look at healthcare and technologies through the lens of patients and physicians via surveys and interviews in order to understand their perspective on digital health, analyse the benefits for them, explore how they can actively engage in the innovation process, and identify the threats and opportunities the large volumes of data create by digitizing healthcare. Are patients truly ready to know everything about their health? What is the value of their data? How can other stakeholders join the patient empowerment movement? This unique perspective will help us re-design the future of healthcare - an industry in desperate need for a change.

Digital Health and Patient Data

Empowering Patients in the Healthcare Ecosystem

Disa Lee Choun
and
Anca Petre

A PRODUCTIVITY PRESS BOOK

First published 2023
by Routledge
605 Third Avenue, New York, NY 10158

and by Routledge
2 Park Square, Milton Park, Abingdon, Oxon, OX14 4RN

Routledge is an imprint of the Taylor & Francis Group, an informa business

Library of Congress Cataloging-in-Publication Data
A catalog record for this title has been requested

ISBN: 9781032105567 (hbk)
ISBN: 9781032105543 (pbk)
ISBN: 9781003215868 (ebk)

DOI: 10.4324/9781003215868

Typeset in Garamond
by SPi Technologies India Pvt Ltd (Straive)

To the patients that never give up and continue to demand for better treatment and care.
To our friends and peers for believing in us.
To our families for their unconditional support.

Contents

Foreword

Who are the patients? No, really, this is a serious question. The word is used by those in healthcare and medicine, but patients don't think of themselves that way – they actually feel more impatient if truth be told. 'Patients' still feel like the people they were five minutes before their diagnosis, and they certainly don't want to be in the situation they face. In fact, once you are labelled a 'patient' it feels like landing onto a foreign planet without a roadmap, a dictionary, or any kind of survival training. I've learned through my varied experiences that it is time to stop blaming patients for their lack of knowledge and place responsibility for effective health literacy in the arms of those collecting, using, and providing data in its many forms. This is why the approach the authors are taking in this book is so critical – find the multiple moments to listen early and often, and practice WIIFP (What's In It For Patients?) at each step of the digital health and data movement to lead us all to better healthcare systems that work more effectively for patients.

My own 'patient' experiences started just after being promoted to a computer company's headquarters to run all their training services for customers and employees. Call it a crash course in clearly explaining data's impact to people and businesses while at the same time dealing with a rude awakening called Stage 3c triple negative breast cancer and learning that the healthcare system is not set up for patients and their needs, at least in the US. In the decades since, healthcare has become even more complicated while the system touts its focus on 'patient centricity' (whatever that means).

While still working 6 days per week, I entered the burgeoning world of breast cancer patient advocacy in the early 1990s. We followed the lead of HIV/AIDS in advocating for ourselves and demanding better answers for our unmet needs. After my husband and I joined the Board of Breast Cancer Action, we quickly traversed through traditional and less traditional modes of patient support, fundraising, lobbying, and 'watchdog' advocacy which firmly stated things that didn't work in healthcare or medicine. After learning more about how disjointed drug and device development operated in academia and the business community, it seemed important to focus attention on fixing that. While expecting a somewhat simple and timely solution, we find ourselves almost 30 years later in a vortex of changes that may or may not create a more results-oriented system for patients and the people they love. We have also experienced multiple medical conditions since our original exposure and have learned first-hand that healthcare issues exist across disease spectrums. One key step to addressing substantive change is for medicine and healthcare to stop inadvertently blaming patients. Healthcare professionals may not realize how endemic this feeling is for patients, but it starts with language like "the patient failed the treatment" which is totally inaccurate. Unfortunately, treatments too often fail patients; not the other way around. There are many more examples of common medical language that blames patients, and which must be reversed if we are to build the trust that must be there for patients to share their data. This means considering patients and their needs for all types, backgrounds, cultures, and races. One of the many topics that Anca and Disa address in the book focuses on building trust to enable data sharing and how this could potentially enable improved applications throughout the healthcare ecosystem.

Patient Advocates In Research (PAIR) has also been helping create these kinds of changes and we're still at it. PAIR is an informal international communication network with hundreds of patient advocates, who are usually members of other patient groups in many diseases and medical conditions. We work with researchers and patient communities, and regularly discuss what research means from a patient perspective and how to translate medical advances into better healthcare. PAIR was formed after it became clear that it didn't matter how much money or legislation was poured into research and product development – we clearly must improve the way research and healthcare systems work and change the mindset of people doing the work. We help researchers and governments approach more multidisciplinary collaborations to build more cohesive, coherent, and comprehensive systems. And most of all, we help them think about how they can impact the lives of people who become patients with medical conditions they address throughout the entire product development lifecycle. This means all patients no matter their age, means, or culture. Digital health and data hold the potential to help break cycles of systemic racism that are built into healthcare if we address them with each project and product. We must consciously include solutions if we truly want to translate the current hyperbole (hype) to reach its potential and empower those we are counting on for support. It is imperative to help people understand what data are, how they can be used for personal benefit versus societal gain, and what kind of risks are involved as we reach towards the idealized goal of more personalized care. Straightforward, plain language that incorporates health literacy principles (including visual and numeracy methods) is imperative to give people the context they need to apply digital and medical options that fit their own needs. This also means that digital solutions need to be anchored in shared decision-making principles and in Patient-Reported Outcomes (PRO) and other patient experience research methods.

The authors thoroughly and carefully analyze the potential and challenges of digital health and data, as you will see throughout this book. I met Disa and Anca through a like-minded colleague named Angus Gunn. Their backgrounds in pharmacy, companies, and data complement each personal 'patient' experience, and add a good blend of expertise to create this book. Through hours of discussion, we quickly agreed that although biopharmaceutical, research, and healthcare worlds tend to listen to patients and people, more needs to be done to allow data and digital health to become a catalyst for change. Change can be a double-edged sword, however, if key issues such as accuracy, interoperability, and privacy are glossed over or are not addressed in thoughtful ways that include patient needs and concerns. It became clear that we share mutual hopes and concerns about data and digital solutions—about how important it is that people learn about their data rights and responsibilities, and that safety measures are put into place to hold those who touch health data accountable for responsible data stewardship. If done well, this can become a win-win situation for all involved – the safer people feel about sharing their data, the more data will be available for those who can turn it into useful solutions for patients and those who care for them. In this way, we may be able to help build healthcare systems that can truly learn from ongoing experiences and improve (aka learning healthcare systems).

Many hurdles stymie the path of patients, healthcare providers, and researchers who want to use data effectively. This book addresses many of them, including (but not limited to) access to different types of data and by whom; ownership of personal data versus databases; and the ability to sustain new treatments that do not bankrupt families or governments. Data are tools, just like biospecimens, clinical records, and other more traditional types of patient information. I'd like to illustrate a particular point here that is touched on in the book but needs further exploration with patients included: the hype surrounding "Real World Data" (RWD) will never become real without careful and strategic standards that build Real World Evidence (RWE) that can be used to develop the Real World Answers (RWA) that patients and those who care for them desire.

The only way to provide RWA is to include everyone who has a stake in this endeavour, especially patients who often stake their very lives into clinical trials and research studies. That includes people like me, who advocate for data sharing efforts and volunteer for studies that explore new digital approaches to build better health solutions. We are counting on all of you to join this digital revolution so real solutions can be developed for many health issues. Glad you are here to learn more from these impressive authors, and welcome! Now, let's get started.

Deborah E. Collyar

Preface

Why do we allow all our private conversations on messaging apps to be recorded by third parties? Why do we accept without a problem that all our movements are monitored as soon as we turn on our GPS? Why do we accept that all our purchases are shared with companies all over the world as soon as we use our credit card? And yet, why is it so hard for us to accept that our health data can be recorded, monitored, or shared?

Perhaps the answer is in the question. As soon as we talk about health, the rules change. What we tolerate in other areas becomes intolerable when it comes to our health. Our health is our most precious asset, and the Covid-19 pandemic taught us all how much we should value it. So, could it be that when it comes to the use of our health data, we have different and/or higher expectations than when it comes to other types of personal data?

When we started writing this book, we wanted to explore the relationship patients have with their health data. In recent years, the conversation has been revolving around the numerous data breaches in hospitals or data misuse by private companies. Because of it, the public debate has been focused mainly on the threats of data sharing and on the restrictive measures that should be put in place to protect personal data. But the reality is not that dark. In fact, it seemed to us that citizens are usually open to the use of their health data when four conditions are met:

1. It is useful to them or to the community
   Most of us accept the use of our personal data when we feel like we are gaining something out of it. For instance, we share information with our doctors because it allows them to make better decisions and improve the care we receive. We also gladly agree to share our health data with Apple when we activate our health app on our smartphone or with Garmin when we count our steps with our smartwatch. The service we receive in exchange for our health data is useful enough for us to accept the use of our personal information. On the contrary, scandals seem to emerge when citizens feel like their health data not only has been used against their will, but it hasn't benefited them in any way.
2. They understand what happens when they share their data
   The way health data is collected, stored, or used is challenging to understand even for professionals working in this field. But for the general public, it must feel like a huge black box. They know by now that a lot of organizations have an interest in gathering their health data but the way this works precisely is a mystery. So, what do people do in the 21st century when they don't understand something? They look it up online. The problem is that online they can find a lot of misleading information that only accentuates their worries and their fear. Educating the public about the use of health data appeared to be a key topic for us to address in this book. This is why we dedicated two chapters to explaining not only what is in this mysterious black box of data processing but also what are some of the applications of

health data that most people have never heard of but that will have a great impact in the future of healthcare.

3. They feel like they have a choice

Then comes the question of choice and this is where the gap widens dramatically between health data and other personal data. For example, I can turn off my GPS so that my movements are not tracked. I can also pay in cash if I don't want my buying behaviour to be scrutinized. But when it comes to health data it feels like we are being held hostage by the system. I'm not going to stop seeking treatment just because I don't want my health data to be used. I have no alternative most of the time. So how can we address this question of choice? Is it simply by creating consent forms each time we want to use health data, or should we think of a more sophisticated system? Actually, what about giving patients full control over their health data? It is one of the key questions we needed to explore in this book.

4. The last element, and arguably one of the most important, is trust. They trust the individual or the organization looking to use their data

Trust is a subjective phenomenon. It is a clever mix of several factors such as the credibility of the organization handling the data. For example, we are more likely to trust a well-known public research organization to conduct studies based on our data than a new tech start-up. Trust is also based on an alignment of interests. If the organization only defends its personal interests, trust is shattered. If our interests are aligned, then trust can be restored. The problem, as you are no doubt aware of, is that in health, there is a real breakdown in that trust. Therefore, one of our missions with this book is to identify some of the trust principles that should be adopted for effective data sharing.

This book also looks at data sharing from a technological perspective. As we are both passionate about the digital transformation of the healthcare industry, we decided to explore the different technologies that can help create the ideal data sharing framework. Whether it is blockchain or federated learning, these technologies pave the way for a more secure and privacy-preserving use of health data.

Finally, this book was also born from the personal experience of being a patient with a rare condition, Devic's disease. This is the story of Disa, who was undiagnosed for 10 years. Going from doctor to doctor, test after test, 'inconclusive' was the only feedback she received. Eventually, getting the right referral but with delays exacerbated the condition from which she never fully recovered and led to chronic pain. Even as a pharmacist and understanding all the drugs and treatments, medical terms, procedures, etc. it was still an exhausting process. Imagine what a person would have to go through if they had no medical type of background or degree and the support they would need to guide them through. Despite Disa's condition, her chronic pain could potentially be avoided but with the advancement of technology and digitalization of health records, there is hope that in the future, patients could have early diagnoses and treatment with the right medication and therapies.

Our passion is to empower patients through digital health. The industry is only at the beginning of this journey. Therefore, it is important to have the right policies in place to ensure that we are making the best use of the citizen's data, abiding by their rights and data privacy laws, and the right level of security. There is so much we can do with the right data, such as using it for advanced analytics, to improve treatments, drug discovery, and more. There is no limit to what we can achieve especially if we, as citizens, collaborate with the healthcare and pharmaceutical industries, with the government and policymakers, with research organizations, and all other stakeholders involved in this space. Look at what we as a global society achieved with the Covid-19 vaccines, ensuring the safety of the population through education, prevention, and care, digital solutions, and devices to measure vital signs including temperature, etc. These are all through health data and the willingness to fight for a common good: a cure.

Acknowledgements

This book would not have been possible without the contribution of our friends and peers. We would like to thank everyone who provided their expertise, input, and shared their passion and the work they continue to do to push the needle in digital health.

In alphabetical order:

Adama Ibrahim
Pharmaceutical Company

Angus Gunn
Fellow at King's College London, Member of Board of directors for Center for Medical Technology Policy, Pharmaceutical Company

Catherine Cerisey
Patient advocate

Craig Lipset
Adviser and Founder of Clinical Innovation Partners, Co-Chair of DTRA, Adjunct Assistant Professor, Department of Health Informatics at Rutgers Biomedical and Health Sciences, Adjunct Instructor at University of Rochester Center for Health and Technology

xxiv ■ *Acknowledgements*

Dan Gebremedhin
Partner at Flare Capital Partners

Dave deBronkart
Chief Patient Officer for PocketHealth; Advisory Board for OpenNotes; Speaker and Author

David Gruson
Health Director at Jouve, Founder of ETHIK-IA

Deborah Collyar
Founder of PAIR

Francesca Rocchi
Hospital Pharmacists

Gabriel Eichler
Pharmaceutical Company

Giuseppe Pontrelli
Hospital Clinician and Researcher

Gloria Kayani
Chief Operating Officer, Thrombosis Research Institute

Gozde Susuzlu
Project coordinator at the European Patients' Forum

Guillaume Marchand
Psychiatrist – Head of university Unit Hélios at Centre Hospitalier Alpes-Isere

Guillemette Jacob
Patient advocate, Founder of Seintinelles

Jesper Kjaer
Director of Data Analytics Centre, Danish Medicines Agency

Mehdi Benchoufi
MD, Maths PHD, co-founder echOpen

Olivier de Fresnoye
CEO at echOpen

Pascal Bouquet
Pharmaceutical Company

Romain Finas
VP Real-World Evidence at Alira Health

Sabina A. Kineen
Patient Advocate

Ségolène Perin
Head of Primary Care Development at ELSAN

Stéphane Sclison
Senior Partner, IQVIA

Notes on the Authors

Disa Lee Choun has been working in the pharmaceutical industry for over 15 years, from leading global initiatives in digital transformation to setting up strategies for digital solutions. She is also an adviser for start-up companies, including non-profit organizations, and assessor for new innovation. Prior to joining the pharmaceutical industry, she was a co-founder of a technology company. She has a pharmacy degree and an EMBA.

Due to her passion in digital health and emerging technologies, in 2019, she was awarded the Top 100 Women in Technology, Financial Times Top 100 Most Influential BAME Leader, and featured on the cover of CIO Look celebrating Women in Tech edition in June 2019.

She current resides in the United Kingdom.

Anca Petre, PharmD, is a digital health entrepreneur passionate about the impact of emerging technologies in healthcare.

Her mission is to detect the latest tech trends in healthcare and raise awareness about their impact on patients. She has worked with major industry players such as pharmaceutical companies, international patient advocacy groups, start-ups, healthcare facilities and public institutions to explore and analyse new technologies and digital solutions. As a TEDx speaker, she travels the world to deliver inspiring and impactful keynotes about the future of healthcare.

Anca completed a double degree in pharmaceutical sciences at Université Paris-Saclay and management at INSEEC Business School. During her PharmD, she specialized in the way blockchain technology can help patients better manage their health data.

Chapter 1

The Patient Empowerment Movement

Medicine and healthcare have a direct impact on our life expectancy and our quality of life. It defines what is health and sickness, and the path we take when we are diagnosed with a medical condition. Medicine is embodied by healthcare professionals, and physicians occupy a central role. They are the carriers of knowledge, hope, and despair. Patients and societies place their trust, their expectations, and their lives in their medical teams. This power has placed physicians on the highest pedestal, but the power balance between doctors and patients has been in constant evolution throughout history. Early medicine was characterized by a strong medical figure dominating the patient. Today, this balance tends to reach an equilibrium. Access to care, information, the deceleration of medical breakthroughs, numerous health scandals, and the recent health crisis have given patients a strong voice and a central role in this health democracy.

DOI:10.4324/9781003215868-1

From a Doctor-Centred Model to a Patient-Centred Model

In 1956, Szasz and Hollender described three types of patient–doctor relationship models: the active-passivity, the guidance-co-operation, and the mutual participation[1]. Even at the end of the 20th century, the patient–doctor relation was a paternalistic one. The patient was merely the subject and recipient of care but had no active role in the interactions with the medical team. Healthcare was doctor-centred but in the last 50 years, an important change developed. Healthcare started becoming more patient-centred and oriented towards a mutual participation model. To understand why it took so long and what fuelled this revolution, it is interesting to take a closer look at the doctor–patient relationship throughout the ages.

Early "medicine" was mainly based on trial and error. Those who mastered the art of mixing plants and differentiating between edible and toxic ones became the first healers. With them, emerged the idea of a knowledgeable parent-figure, capable of helping and curing others. But their role was not limited to finding remedies in plants. It also encompassed a mystical approach. Sickness was sometimes seen as a supernatural intervention, and healers were attributed supernatural powers to cure the sufferers. The expression of their powers was linked to beliefs, talismans, and rituals. As such, early medicine was a mix of science, magic, and folklore. Healers had a strong influence based on the knowledge gap created with others. Although this dynamic emerged thousands of years ago, it has profoundly impacted the patient–doctor relationship and society's vision of healthcare professionals up until today. It is worth noting that from the very early days of medicine, the difference between the healers and the others was based on knowledge. Those who knew had the power versus those who didn't know.

The first disruption in Western medicine came with the Greek civilization. They were among the first to include empirical observations and experimentations in the practice of medicine and move away from magical and religious considerations. The most famous Greek physician, Hippocrates, is considered as "the father of Western medicine". His famous oath described the patient not only as a recipient of care but also as a human whose rights and privacy ought to be respected. Medical ethics were born, and the doctor–patient relationship began its transformation.

Despite the period of Greek enlightenment, for centuries to come, depending on the social and political context of a given time, the relationship between doctors and patients went back and forth between the active-passive and the guidance-cooperation. Paintings ranging from the 17th to the 19th centuries represented elegantly dressed father figures surrounding a patient often laid out on a bed and submissively receiving care. Much like a parent looking over their child, the doctor's role was to act in the patient's best interest and make the necessary decisions.

By the late 19th century, the rise of psychology encouraged physicians to look past their patients' physical symptoms and further interact with them, understand their experience, and create a genuine relationship based on communication. In 1964, Dr. Michael Balint described the idea of "mutual investment" where both doctors and patients have an active role in building a trust relationship. In the following years, a large body of literature was written to explore and advocate for a more patient-centred approach of medicine. Seeing the patient as a person rather than a superposition of biomedical phenomena rapidly led to a multifactorial vision of care. Doctors understood that the same diseases can be experienced in diametrically opposed ways depending on the patient. Financial, cultural, social, or political considerations need to be taken into account.

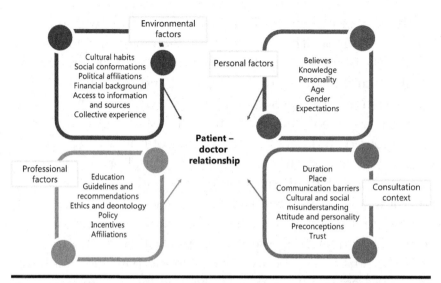

Figure 1.1   The components of the patient–doctor relationship.

These factors are known as the social determinants of health (refer to Chapter 2), they help understand a patient's uniqueness and individuality (Figure 1.1).

MINI CASE STUDY 1.1:   A PATIENT'S PERSPECTIVE ON THE DOCTOR–PATIENT RELATIONSHIP

To better understand the dynamic between doctors and patients, we talked with several patients and patient advocates, including Catherine Cerisey, a French patient advocate. Her standpoint helped us better understand where the doctor–patient relationship truly stands in countries such as France.

In France, there has always been an opposition between patients and health professionals due to medical paternalism. Doctors consider they know everything about their patients: they know what they think, what they want, what they believe. But patients are fully capable of understanding their situation and give their consent for their own care.

Thankfully, we are not in opposition with all doctors and some of them have very well understood the benefit of working in partnership with patients, whether individually or through advocacy groups. But we want all doctors to understand that patients can be valuable partners and contribute to care in other ways than by simply giving their consent. We should always aim for a shared decision-making relationship in which patients and doctors discuss the best care. Patients and doctors can both exchange information whether it is from their experience or from scientific studies to ultimately reach a consensus, that it is mutually beneficial. If patients are empowered to choose the best care in accordance with their lifestyle and the doctor's expertise and medical knowledge, chances are they will be way more adherent to their treatment. If patients don't have a say in their care, they are less likely to follow through. We can compare this paternalistic relationship to that between a child and their parent. If you force a kid to read a book instead of watching TV, chances are they will refuse. But if you take the kid to a bookstore and help them pick a book they like, they will most likely decide to read it because they were part of the decision-making process.

Catherine's comment about treatment adherence made us think about a remark from Deborah Collyar, founder of Patient Advocates In Research (PAIR). She explained to us that only the medical, research and regulatory communities think of it as "adherence or compliance". From a patient perspective, we talk about "endurance". This changes the whole approach, and we can come up with better ways to help patients incorporate their medical priorities into the rest of their lives.

Continuing our discussion with Catherine, we realized that the paternalistic patient–doctor relationship is very close to a teen–parent relationship, with the benefits and challenges it can create. Just as parents, doctors consider "they know best" and are therefore entitled to make decisions of behalf of their patients, with their best interest at heart. But if you are a parent yourself, you know well that imposing your way of thinking soon has its limits. Teenagers can start hiding information from you because they fear they will be grounded or mocked. According to Catherine, the same applies to patients, that tend to be less transparent with their health provider if they fear that it will trigger a negative reaction.

Catherine provides us with an example of this paternalistic approach taken to an extreme:

In the context of sleep apnoea, I came across patients that had their continuous positive airway pressure (CPAP) machines removed from them if they weren't adherent to their treatment. It is just like saying that you remove a patient's medication if he doesn't take it according to the prescription. The correct approach would be to support the patient in using the machine correctly and adapt the use to their lifestyle and their needs. Not just punish them if they don't comply.

In our interview with Deborah Collyar, she said:

> We need to stop blaming patients when their treatments aren't successful. They don't fail treatments, treatments fail patients. If we want to build trust, we should have patients as partners. In order to achieve that, you can't start by blaming them for their own disease. It's endemic in medicine and research, a kind shorthand that is actually inaccurate, and we need to stop it.

Another patient I met during an event about artificial intelligence (AI) also had an interesting perspective on his relationship with his doctors. As we were at an AI event, we started discussing the importance of having large and good quality data sets to train AI models. As such, patients have a responsibility in making sure the information they provide their health professionals is as accurate as possible because it might end up being used to create AI. To this end, the patient I was talking to added an interesting comment:

> I would like to be told if the information I give my doctor is used to train AI models. If it is, I will make sure it is as reliable and complete as possible. If not, then I might not put so much effort in providing good quality information to my doctor especially if I fear they might judge my habits or that it might not be relevant to the conversation.

Interestingly, this patient was saying that he would be much more transparent with a machine than with a doctor. This anecdote illustrates the importance of creating a balanced and trustworthy relationship with patients because, despite a doctor's best efforts at gathering accurate information, patients are not always open to giving it out if they feel it can play against them. In addition, talking to our interviewees, especially in the US, there are data errors in their health records where patients sometimes are not able to have them fixed. These data errors can do harm for example wrong medication and dosing. This highlights the importance for patients and their health providers or doctors to work together and ensure that data are as accurate as possible.

Setting Rights, Sharing Knowledge, Defining New Rules

The end of the 20th century marked another crucial moment in the evolution of patients' role in healthcare. Up until then, much of the discussion was centred on how to create a more balanced and mutually beneficial patient–doctor relationship. But starting with the second half of the 20th century, the spectrum of considerations widened to reconsider the patient's role within the entire health system.

The First Patient Movements

Patient movements started in the 50s, became well known in the 80s with the AIDS epidemic, and have continued to this day.[2] Patient involvement has taken on unprecedent significance. From supporting one-another through advocacy groups, to organizing fundraising activities for research, to lobbying for more patient-oriented regulations, to participating in drafting clinical trials protocols, patients felt the need to regain control over the health system they were supposed to benefit from. They played an increasing role on three aspects of healthcare: the production and diffusion of medical knowledge (initially reserved to the scientific and medical communities), the direction in which medical research evolved, and the development of new health policies.

The first AIDS activists influenced the way society looks at patients and the importance given to their point of view. This movement started when gay communities in the United States felt threatened by a disease of high mortality and surrounded by stigma. A disease that often led to what sociologists called "social death", referring to AIDS patients being considered as-good-as-dead as soon as they fell ill. Although AIDS activism started in gay communities, it soon influenced many communities living with AIDS across the world as it spread to all lifestyles. This led, in 1983, to the Denver Principles, a framework for patient empowerment that launched a global movement.

The principles, written by a group called "People With AIDS", set rights and recommendations for healthcare professionals, patients, and all those concerned by the epidemic. What initially seemed like a small gathering of people sharing their experience, rapidly became an illustration of the power patients can hold and deploy when their needs aren't satisfied. The rights claimed for people with AIDS became universal rights for all patients. Among them, patients with AIDS have the right to full explanations of all medical procedures and risks, to choose or refuse their treatment modalities, to refuse to participate in research without jeopardizing their treatment and to make informed decisions about their lives. They also have the right to privacy and to confidentiality of medical records.

Along with AIDS, other diseases such as breast cancer benefited from patient movements that transformed individual health issues into collective fights. As an example, Eleanor Pred, a breast cancer patient founded Breast Cancer Action (BCA), a San Francisco Bay Area organization destined to help women seek information about their disease and its treatments. She started the grassroots movement in the US in the early 1990s that later founded the National Breast Cancer Coalition (NBCC). Eleanor herself struggled to find reliable data on her metastatic disease from unresponsive health organizations. Deborah Collyar, an active patient advocate and past board member of BCA shared her experience with us during an interview:

> I was diagnosed with cancer at 32. I left my job and joined Breast Cancer Action where my husband and I both became board members, thanks to Eleanor Pred. The world of patient advocacy is made of five different puzzle pieces: direct to patient support, fund raising, political advocacy, watchdog, and research advocacy. Our focus is advocating for patients in research to make it more relevant and to achieve better results for patients.

In the early patient movements one common concept emerges: patients need to be self-sovereign. And self-sovereignty can only be accomplished if the knowledge gap between medical communities and patients is reduced.

Reducing the Knowledge Gap

Two of the most important needs patients have included are the production of knowledge about their disease and the receipt of information to make informed choices about their health. Creating a doctor–patient alliance requires creating a two-way flow of information: from doctors to patients as a way of informing, educating, reassuring, and raising awareness and from patients to doctors as a way of providing insights about what happens "in real life". As such, patients and patient associations play a growing role in producing medical knowledge based on their personal experience to accelerate research and better adapt their care. In exchange, some patients expect to be included in decision-making processes and to have access to all the information they deem necessary to understand their health and the care they receive. But where does this information come from? Is it given to patients by doctors? To some extent, yes, as healthcare professionals have a responsibility to inform their patients. But rarely is that enough, so patients start searching for information elsewhere. And these days, elsewhere is the Internet.

Since the beginning of the 21st century and the rollout of the Internet, scientific papers have been exploring how access to online information can impact the doctor–patient relationship and the way patients view and accept care. Some studies suggest that nearly all patients use the Internet to fact-check information provided by the medical team, independent of the level of trust they place in health professionals.[3] Others conclude that if patients trust their doctor, information sought online won't have a significant impact on their relationship.[4] One thing is certain, easy access to mobile devices worldwide coupled with inexpensive connectivity turned the Internet into the number-one source of medical information. 70% of adults in the world search for health-related information online.[5] It is important to educate the public and create awareness, increasing the health and digital literacy to use legitimate health sites for example from healthcare or government agencies, hospitals, clinics, patient advocacy, and scientific research sites. It is critical to help patients learn quickly how to spot misinformation that could actually harm them.

Examples of both beneficial and detrimental use of the Internet exist. A 2018 study by Jones et al.[6] explores the public perception of brain death by performing simple Google and YouTube searches for the keyword "brain death". As expected, the quality of the information varies from one source to another. 40% of Google websites and 60% of

YouTube videos analyzed during the study contained misleading information, inconsistent with national guidelines. One-third of the videos even included negative comments towards the medical community. But more worrying is the fact that seemingly scientific and medical sources provide incomplete or inaccurate information. This only creates more confusion and incomprehension and affects the public's ability to make informed and rational decisions.

Similar examples can easily be found. The Covid-19 pandemic even coined the term "infodemic" to describe this tsunami of fake news: "Vaccines contain microchips", "Covid-19 can be cured with vitamin C", "Place an onion in your room to catch the Covid-19 germs". This is even more worrying when knowing that up to 26% of videos on YouTube about Covid-19 were misleading[7] and that 90 million warning labels were put on Facebook content because it was inaccurate or false, during March and April 2020 alone.[8] Even more researchers warn about the impact such information has on individuals and on public health: purchase habits are modified (e.g. people rushed to buy masks or even toilet paper in some countries), drugs can be used in harmful ways, mental health is deteriorated. In other words, misinformation can have a life-threatening effect and creates a bigger divide between healthcare systems, government, and the public.

Although recently the focus has been on the harm the Internet can cause, talking to patients, we realized that the Internet also helped a lot of them and even contributed to saving their lives.

The story of Dave deBronkart, also known as e-patient Dave, is a great example to illustrate the power of patient empowerment through technology. In 2007, Dave was diagnosed with stage IV, grade 4 metastatic renal cell carcinoma, a very aggressive form of cancer. Desperately, he browsed the web in search for information, support, and solutions. His doctor suggested him to sign up to the ACOR community, a group of cancer patients and caregivers, which became his number-one source of reliable information. By talking to other members of the community, he discovered that there is a treatment for his cancer, but it only works on a small number of patients and most hospitals don't even offer it. He eventually succeeded in receiving this treatment that ended up saving his life.[9] That was one of the first steps he took to take control over his health using the Internet. In the following weeks, he continued to search and ask for more information online. He used PatientSite, a website that gives patients access to their medical records and visit notes, to go through all his data and share it with qualified friends and relatives. He downloaded his hospital data to put it in an Excel spreadsheet to keep track of it himself. Finally, he started sharing his journey and supporting others through his own blog. As he put it himself during our interview, "patients are the ultimate stakeholders", meaning that no one else has more at stake than a patient whose life or wellbeing is threatened. Online information becomes a powerful tool for patients wanting to better understand their condition, find therapeutic alternatives, or share their experience.

More recently, in 2017, Andre Kushniruk, editor-in-chief of JMIR Human Factors and health informatics specialist, was diagnosed with advanced stage tongue cancer.[10] Initially, his surgeon told him his tumour was too large to be operated on and that he only had a slim chance to survive beyond two years. But Kushniruk and his wife took matters into their own hands and researched using the Internet to verify the surgeon's assessment. Information found in the academic literature and on patient blogs showed them that there could be another way. Within weeks, he was able to schedule an appointment with a specialist in New York and receive the life-saving surgery. Had it not been for the information available online, the outcome might have been completely different.

Of course, these examples only represent personal experiences and don't reflect the way all patients feel. It is important to have a complete representation of what patients go through and help them understand that their input and participation is always important. Nevertheless, such examples are becoming more and more common. In the US, 18% of patients look for peers with the same health problem online.[11] Among the reasons why patients' communities are attracting an increasing number of users is the fact that they provide educational resources, feedback on care strategies, and emotional support. For example, a survey conducted on Proud2BeMe,[12] a website and community for patients suffering from eating disorders, showed that users felt empowered by the information they accessed, the ability to share their experience and the recognition they found online.

Access to information appears to be the number one patient empowerment tool. Given that throughout history the paternalistic patient–doctor relationship has mainly been based on a knowledge gap, bridging that gap with information available online is disrupting health. Patients are not the end recipients of care anymore; they are active contributors to their health. This new dynamic is further fuelled by the boom in digital health services that provide patients with solutions and alternatives outside of the medical world. Although some health professionals still struggle to adapt to this new dynamic, the knowledge gap may continue to decrease in upcoming years, as qualitative and reliable information becomes more and more accessible. Notably, we also need to point out the socioeconomic factors that affects access to care and information. Unfortunately, this is still an issue for many disenfranchised communities, especially BAME (Black Asian and Minority Ethnic).

Creating a New Doctor–Patient Relationship Framework

The first step in creating a doctor–patient relationship is understanding how access to online health information changes the patient's behaviour.

In 2019, 'Doctor Google' received over 1 billion health-related requests every day. That is over 70,000 requests per minute, comprising approximately 7% of the total volumes of requests on the search engine.[13] In parallel, given the number of doctors worldwide and the average number of patients they see, there are roughly 92 million doctor's appointments daily in the world. These data show that every day, 10 times as many people look for health information online than go to see a health professional. Online searches even spike in the weeks before patients visit an ER,[14] and 1 in 3 patients research treatment options online before a doctor's appointment.[15] In other words, the Internet has become the antechamber of medicine.

Browsing information online is often correlated with higher levels of confusion and anxiety, especially in patients unable to evaluate the reliability and quality of the source. Some studies suggest that up to one-third of respondents felt anxious after reading health-related information online.[16] In contrast, one-quarter of these same respondents felt relieved.

The complexity emerges when patients present their findings to their health professionals. A feeling of uneasiness can appear if doctors fail to acknowledge the information and have a defensive response. This can irreversibly damage the patient-provider relationship and leave patients feeling misunderstood and confused between the divergent sources of information. But trust can be broken to even greater degrees. If the relationship deteriorates with their health providers, patients may discontinue their care. In one study, 11% of respondents affirmed stopping their treatment because of information found online (which may or may not have been accurate).[17] Other studies show that, on the contrary, most patients tend to make pro-health decisions as a consequence of accessing health-relation information online: making doctor appointments (45%), asking questions about their treatment or their diagnosis (40%), or undergoing additional tests (35%).

Today, doctors are expected to guide patients towards reliable sources and be open to discussing the information found online. Helping a patient use critical thinking approaches and pointing them to appropriate resources can contribute to more empowered and informed decisions about their health. But encouraging patients to educate themselves also means, for physicians, accepting that they might come across information contradictory with the current treatment plan. Patients on the other hand, need to understand that unless a doctor is very specialized in a particular disease, chances are they will not be aware of all the latest research available on the topic. This is where the patient–doctor partnership needs to be productive: clinicians might have to address their patient to a more specialized colleague and patients need to accept some of the limits of the medical practice and act constructively.

Studies also show that often patients need health providers to explain and contextualize the information available online. They seek reassurance more than they question the skills and the knowledge of the medical team. Addressing this need alone can reinforce the doctor–patient relationship and allow patients to feel more considered and involved in their own care.[18] An increasing need for health literacy demands better access to information for patients and communication skills for healthcare providers.

Online communities and resources can provide patients with disease-specific information, emotional support, and real-life experiences. They can also help patients learn how they go about receiving the best care that's available to them according to the latest studies. Combined with the medical expertise and the guidance of their health providers, patients can hence benefit from the best of both worlds.

Reaching the Mutual Participation Model

Ever since the health crisis that marked the end of the 20th century, patients took a more active role in their care. Empowered by greater access to information, they were able to slowly bridge the knowledge gap between patients and the medical community. But does this necessarily mean that a mutual participation model has been reached?

The mutual participation model, as first described by Szasz and Hollender in 1956, presents the doctor–patient relationship as a partnership in which patients are encouraged to be active participants in their own care. But participation can be defined in many ways, from simply being informed to being empowered.

The International Association for Public Participation (IAP²) created the Spectrum of Public Participation[19] that defines different levels of public participation that can be transposed to patient participation in healthcare. IAP² is an international organization advocating for citizen participation in matters that affect the public interest. Founded in 1990, its initial mission was to involve citizens in governmental and industrial decisions that affected their lives. The Spectrum of Public Participation, although developed for public participation across all topics, can easily be adapted to healthcare (Figure 1.2)[20]:

- Level 1 – Inform: patients are provided information about their health status and the care plan designed for them. They are encouraged to seek further information if needed and health professionals are at their disposal to answer any questions or doubts.

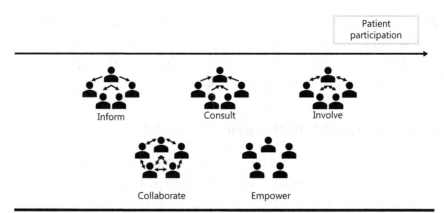

Figure 1.2   The spectrum of patient participation.

- Level 2 – Consult: patients are asked for their feedback and their experience. A two-way flow of information is created. Patients are valued for the knowledge they acquire about their disease and their perception can influence the course of care.
- Level 3 – Involve: patients are involved in the decision-making processes and their feedback is actively sought and considered when adapting care. Their input can be requested during traditional doctor visits but also through collaborative workshops or surveys.
- Level 4 – Collaborate: patients become knowledgeable advisers whose opinions are considered in each step of the health journey. They are equal partners in their own care, but they can also contribute to the design of new study protocols and influence research. At this level, patients are often involved in advisory boards and have an active governance role.
- Level 5 – Empower: patients are the ultimate decision-maker when it comes to their health. They are knowledgeable about their situation and trusted with making the best decision for themselves. This is the ultimate level of self-sovereignty.

When looking at these levels, one can easily deduce from personal experience that Level 5 is very rarely reached. Although this is the goal of many patient advocates and sometimes the claim of health providers, in practice a truly balanced relationship in which patients are considered as equals and sovereign over their health is still an exception. Often, patient participation is somewhere between Levels 1 to 3 depending on the country and on health providers. The few examples of patient empowerment often depicted in the media and presented in this book should not hide most situations in which patients still have a passive role. Nor should this discussion give the feeling that all patients want to be empowered or are given access to do so. Some prefer placing all their trust in their medical team and receive the least information possible. "To each its role" some would say, considering that when it comes to medicine, some patients should be given the choice to remain passive and follow the expert's advice or become the e-patients (Figure 1.3).

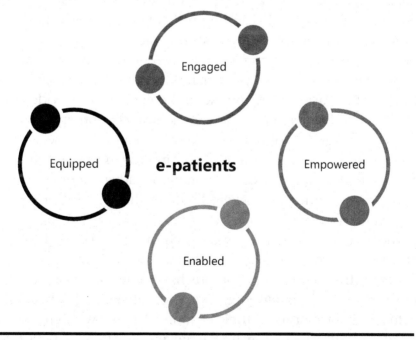

Figure 1.3   e-Patients.

For those who aspire to a more balanced patient–doctor relationship, a collaboration or empowerment model can sometimes seem unachievable. Levels 4 and 5 are far harder to reach as they require a shift in the power structure of healthcare. They demand a shared decision-making process and joint governance. Despite significant enthusiasm and effort to empower patients in speeches and papers, in practice, mentalities and cultures evolve slowly. In the scientific literature, the "patient revolution" is sometimes depicted as an insurrection against an elite or an effort to reverse the balance of power. For instance, the British Medical Journal (BMJ), one of the leading scientific journals in the world and among the firsts to advocate for patient empowerment, can sometimes reflect an ambiguous image of what this revolution entails. In 1999, the cover of the BMJ titled "Embracing patient partnership" depicted a man and a woman dancing a tango, a dance known for its intensity and for the domination battle it enacts. Again, in 2013, an entirely red cover titled "Let the patient revolution begin" and represented a patient's fist raised, using imagery from socialist revolutions, in which the people turned against an elite. Despite encouraging titles and hopeful conclusions, the partnership model still creates a feeling of unease among the medical community, as evidenced by outdated language used by the medical community.

Yet, the benefits of patient empowerment are no secret. From better treatment adherence to improved outcomes, many studies have explored the tangible advantages of a partnership model. Empowered patients have a greater sense of control and responsibility over their health.[21] This is particularly true when it comes to chronic diseases, which affect one in three adults worldwide.[22] Indeed, patients suffering from chronic conditions have time to educate themselves, gain experience and practical skills, and become valuable contributors to their health.[23] Patients with chronic conditions also focus towards achieving a better quality of life rather than finding a cure. As Deborah Collyar says: "We've led the public and patients to believe in "the cure" when in reality, it may not exist. That's why I often say the "C" word isn't "cancer", for instance. It's "cure". There are many things that can be done for patients to help them live better and even longer lives without focusing on a misguided and often misleading concept". Another reason for it is that the healthcare and pharmaceutical industries continue to focus on treating symptoms and pursuing the "cure" rather than targeting the cause of these conditions. For example, investments in gene therapy, which may provide closer views to a cure, are only now becoming viable. Today, science and technology are converging at a pace that will certainly accelerate this race to cures in the near future. Patients, as advocates for these new treatments, will not conform to just receiving the average symptomatic treatment, that might only delay the inevitable and exacerbate the costs of healthcare. The shift to achieving a better quality of life can certainly be accomplished through medical interventions, but it also heavily relies on personal initiative and self-management. Hence, patient involvement is as important in achieving positive outcomes as medical care, whether or not "cure" is possible. Take the well-documented example of diabetes. Studies show that empowered patients are more likely to successfully manage their blood glucose and make effective lifestyle changes. When they do, secondary complications that require hospitalizations decrease, automatically reducing costs, and improving outcomes.[24] Similarly, studies show that in patients with pain and bone metastasis, informed and engaged patients were prescribed more appropriate treatments and had lower pain intensity scores.[25] These are examples of improved physical outcomes that have nothing to do with cure, but the psychological benefits are equally impressive: less fear and anxiety, more self-confidence, and a feeling of hope.[26]

Just as the AIDS epidemic marked a pivotal moment in the fight for patients' rights, the Covid-19 pandemic could help the medical community embrace the partnership model. In times of crisis, all support is welcomed whether it comes from qualified health professionals or from patients themselves. When hospitals were saturated, clinicians were compelled to rely on their patients to manage their own health and take a more active role in their care. Experience and even expertise in health was found as much inside hospitals as outside. It is the joint efforts of the medical and scientific communities, along with patients, the private sector, and public institutions that helped overcome the most important health crisis of the 21st century. When there are no other alternatives than collaborating, mentalities change, and new trust alliances are built with the hope that they will last past the storm.

From Informed Patients to e-Patients

Giving patients access to information is only the first step in empowering them. It certainly creates a more balanced patient-provider relationship and a two-way flow of information, but it doesn't allow patients to fully take control over their health.

One of the leaders of the patient empowerment movement was Dr Tom Ferguson. He was among the first to advocate for patients to inform themselves and to take control over their health with the help of digital tools such as the Internet. Although they are just a minority of patients, he called this new group "e-patients". They are not "just" informed patients. They are equipped, engaged, empowered, enabled:

- e for equipped because e-patients have at their disposal digital tools to manage their health.
- e for engaged because patients are involved in their own care.

- e for empowered because access to digital tools also gives them access to data that allows them to better understand their health.
- e for enabled because data also enables patients to make informed decisions and act in their best interest.

In 1975, Dr Ferguson started writing about the empowered medical consumer and in 1996 he published a book titled "Health online: how to find health information, support groups, and self-help communities in cyberspace". In November 2000, in a paper published in the British Medical Journal,[27] he told the story of Karen Parles, a 38-year-old woman diagnosed with lung cancer who sought support and information online. In that same paper, he described the emergence of tech-savvy patients, able to search for information online and create resources for others. He also anticipated the upheaval it will soon have on the doctor–patient relationship and encouraged clinicians to be open-minded and collaborate with patients rather than feeling threatened. An advice that is still applicable today, over 20 years after. Dr Tom Ferguson was a visionary and one of the first advocates for a better relationship between knowledgeable patients and medical professionals. Before passing in 2006, Dr Ferguson started writing the e-Patient White Paper that encompassed his vision. After his death, his colleagues from the e-Patient Scholars Working Group finished the paper and, in 2009, created the Society for Participatory Medicine.

Equipping e-Patients

As defined by Dr Tom Ferguson, e-patients are, among other things, equipped with digital tools that empower them to learn more about their own health. Apart from traditional information websites and online patients' communities, such tools can include telemedicine platforms, smartphone apps, wearables, or voice assistants.

Telehealth has been a critical tool during the Covid-19 pandemic. Its use increased 78 times[28] during the first months of the crisis, as patients and clinicians sought safer ways to receive and provide care, outside of hospitals. Since then, access to telehealth services stabilized at a level 38 times higher than before Covid-19. What first appeared as a temporary practice in the absence of traditional care, now seems to become common between both physicians and patients. But telehealth is not limited to remote consultations. It encompasses a wide range of remote practices that allow patients to receive care without having to physically see a doctor. For instance, during the pandemic, many companies developed remote monitoring apps for patients that couldn't receive care in a traditional setting but still required a medical follow-up. This was the case in chronic diseases such as diabetes where patients needed support in adjusting their insulin dosage and monitoring their blood sugar. Through apps, patients were able to fill in all their information manually or automatically, for their medical team to track daily. Should inconsistencies or problems appear, the medical team would immediately be put in contact with the patient to take the necessary measures. This type of services provided patients with a sense of security knowing that although they cannot visit their doctor, a medical team is still checking on their health remotely. These were also the kind of services that many patient advocates have pushed for over the last few decades.

Some say that the Covid-19 pandemic had the effect of 10 years of continuous innovation within only a few months. Whether that is true or not remains to be defined, but it undoubtedly accelerated the adoption of many digital tools by forcing patients and health providers to create new habits. Eventually, these changes might have happened anyway, but the pandemic had a catalyzing effect by almost completely shutting down traditional health services and by removing barriers to innovation.

This booming effect took place in many health-related markets. For instance, 527 million wearables were sold in 2020 versus 384 million in 2019.[29] This massive adoption was driven by the consumer's need to monitor their health. Thermometers and oximeters were unsurprisingly the best sellers as fever and desaturation were common in Covid-19 patients. But the health wearables market was already growing before the pandemic. Smartwatches capable of doing an ECG, sleep tracking headbands, or intelligent rings, many connected objects appeared in the health and wellness space. Along with them, patients were given access to mountains of data that was once only available to health professionals. Once again, after the Internet, wearables were providing patients with knowledge about their health.

There are many stories about patients seeking medical assistance after their wearables indicated something was wrong. For instance, in 2015, a high school football player was rushed to the hospital after his smartwatch detected an abnormally high heart rate.[30] During the training, the player felt unwell, and checked his newly bought watch. It showed him that his heart rate was double the normal value, so he went to see his coach and the school's health centre who decided to take him to the ER. He was then diagnosed with rhabdomyolysis, a condition in which muscles break down and flood the blood with toxic proteins. It can cause irreversible damage to organs if it isn't treated on time. Luckily, the football player received the appropriate care and was able to return to a normal life after a couple of days.

Smartwatches, through the data they collect, can also help physicians make the right treatment choices. In New Jersey, a man checked into a hospital's ER after suffering a seizure. His heart rate was oscillating so doctors suspected he had atrial fibrillation, a form of cardiac arrhythmia. To treat him, they needed to know for how long the heart had been beating irregularly. This is when they noticed that the man was wearing a smartwatch. After looking at the data recorded by the wearable, they were able to assess that the heart had been acting up for the past 3 hours and pick the correct treatment.

It's important to note that not all wearables are designed as medical devices and might not have the right certification or qualifications that would provide accurate data. Today, many connected objects are nothing more than wellness gadgets that are not designed to influence health decisions and should not represent medical use for the user. Among them are fitness trackers that often provide information about the number of steps the user takes daily or the average heart rate. For a healthy individual, using these devices doesn't expose to any risk and the data they provide only orient lifestyle choices. However, the situation is entirely different if they are used by a patient suffering, for example, from hypertension. If the heart rate tracker is not reliable enough, the patient might be led into thinking that his disease is evolving. Even though using wearables might inform the patients and physicians that ranges might be outside of the norm, it's always advisable to consult with a physician and do further tests before making any health-related decision.

Another empowering digital service is the availability of electronic health records (EHR) directly to patients through patient portals. Many countries are heavily investing in creating EHRs, driven by new legislation or regulatory frameworks, as we will further discuss in Chapter 4. In 2019, in the US, more than 95% of hospitals were equipped with an EHR.[31] Making these records accessible to patients provides them with comprehensive information about their health through discharge summaries, notes, or lab tests. Movements such as OpenNotes[32] promote greater sharing and transparency between health professionals and patients on medical notes which is critical to ensure accuracy and build trust. Patient access to their medical records was found to have a multitude of positive outcomes from improving medication adherence, to creating more trust in the medical community, to reducing hospitalizations.[33] Countries such as France or the UK have already shared initiatives to make medical records accessible to patients to increase transparency and promote individual responsibility that should help to achieve a more efficient health system.

Digital solutions are slowly creating a parallel medical society, driven by educated patients, empowered to make their own medical decisions based on data provided by smart connected medical devices. For instance, patients who experience trouble sleeping can use a connected headband to track their sleeping patterns and identify irregularities. They can then directly reach out to a specialized health professional to receive the appropriate care based on the data collected through the tracker. A couple of years ago, these same patients would have first consulted their general practitioner to complain about sleeping troubles. They would have then been addressed to a specialist that would have run tests to quantify the problem before finally creating a treatment plan. Wearables can empower patients to create their "à la carte" healthcare journey, outside of traditional pathways. Equipped patients may be more effective and efficient in their care. They can identify the specialists they believe they should see and provide them straight away with reliable data. Empowered patients can lead to good use of public and private resources and decrease the healthcare cost as long as they have quality information and objective help to assess their alternatives.

e-Patients Break the Status Quo

Most digital innovation in healthcare today enters in the field of remote care. This trend, accelerated by the pandemic, encompasses all technologies and techniques that allow patients to manage their health and receive care outside of traditional health facilities. For a very long time, patients mainly expected three things when it came to their care: faster, more affordable, and better care. Today, these expectations are evolving, and new generations are increasingly dissatisfied with traditional health services.[34] According to a 2019 Accenture study, they expect more effectiveness, efficiency, convenience, and transparency in their care. Most of them start relying more on non-traditional health services such as virtual care (39%), on-demand care (19%) or digital therapeutics (12%). Even the choice of health providers is influenced by their level of digitization. Patients will more likely see a doctor that can provide remote monitoring and video consults.

Increasingly, patients are looking for more comfort and a better customer experience. This trend is accentuated by the emergence of new remote services developed by tech companies and health start-ups. Apple has entered the health space at full speed with the Apple Watch and the Health app. Google or Amazon created a variety of at-home medical services such as voice health assistants or AI-based solutions for the fast diagnosis of dermatological diseases. Health tech start-ups create test kits for a multitude of biomarkers that represent an alternative to traditional lab tests. Others focus on building all-in-one medical devices that measure your temperature, can be used as a stethoscope and can perform ECGs. We are already seeing the trend where patients are able to manage their health and receive care from the comfort of their home, while being able to interact with the best health professionals when needed. Will this trend grow and become the new norm?

Unlike other breakthroughs in healthcare, this new wave of digital innovation is created or supported by patients. Patients want information about their health in real time. They are the ones purchasing and using wearables, they subscribe to telehealth services, they interact with virtual assistants and so on. It's a shift of paradigm, they don't wait for a doctor's appointment, but they are proactively using digital solutions and using Internet to become more educated about their health and wellness to a certain extent. It's also important to note that the volume of information could be overwhelming and it's important to use trustworthy sources of information and understand the accuracy of digital solutions that might measure vital signs and others.

Technology is creating a bottom-up system in which patients are the instigators of change. Up until now, healthcare was designed as a pyramidal system, with doctors placed above patients and a top-down flow of information and care. This new system stems from two major transformations in the healthcare system. First, the number of major therapeutic breakthroughs has decreased, often called "me too" treatments that don't add value to patients.[35] Lately, very few discoveries could be described as having the same magnitude as the discovery of antibiotics, blood transfusions, or vaccines. Most therapeutic innovations today have an impact on specific diseases or sub-populations. Partly this is due to new technologies and advancements in science that let us understand the disease better and develop more targeted approaches. We are slowly moving towards more personalized medicine where treatments may be adapted to each individual rather than the entire population.

Second, in contrast, the number of technological breakthroughs in healthcare has skyrocketed. Robotic surgery, artificial intelligence, 3D printing, these new tools have a ripple effect in almost all the corners of the world. At the same time, they have changed the balance of power. Indeed, as discussed above, technology provides patients with access to more knowledge about themselves, their disease, and the system around them. Technology empowers them to seek treatment outside health facilities and connect with other patients. They are not fully dependent on their doctors to receive information and care anymore. Moreover, while scientific advances emerged from the medical community, technological breakthroughs are driven by customer adoption. This also contributes to potentially creating a more balanced patient–doctor relationship in which both sides contribute to better health outcomes. For the first time in history, patients are empowered both by knowledge and concrete tools.

From Health Literacy to eHealth Literacy: Opportunities and Challenges

Up until now, patients mainly had access to information about their health through online resources that presented data from studies, or personal experiences from other patients. Today, patients have access, through technology, to data about themselves. In addition to looking for "what works for people like me", they can start investigating "what works for me". But just as a house filled with books doesn't make someone smart, access to data doesn't make patients knowledgeable about their health. Between data and knowledge is the capacity to interpret information. This is called data literacy. By analogy, children can only interpret a series of letters placed one after the other once they learn how to read. Patients also need to learn how to make sense of medical information to create a positive impact on their health.

Through the first part of this chapter, we discussed the fact that access to information empowered patients to take more control over their health. What we failed to point out however, is that access to information is not enough. Patients must make a significant effort to understand the information, adapt it to their case and draw appropriate conclusions. Whether it is online information or information provided by the medical staff, patients need to "translate" it into simple terms to fully understand it. This reminds us of some of our friends that used to record their medical appointments so we could listen and "translate" what the doctor was saying. Similar things happen with online information, despite efforts to simplify complex medical jargon. By doing the effort of adapting the medical content to their understanding, patients acquire a certain level of health literacy.

Health literacy was defined by the US government's 'Healthy People 2030' initiative as "the degree to which individuals have the ability to find, understand, and use information and services to inform health-related decisions and actions for themselves and others."[36] Today, more than half of Americans have a low level of health literacy.[37] It is noteworthy that health literacy doesn't only include the capacity to understand information. It also encompasses the ability to use that information to make informed health decisions. This is the "push and pull" system, where citizens demand for access to information in plain language and organizations including government agencies to need pre-empt the best way to disseminate the information that could be easily consumed by the public.

Previous studies showed that low health literacy is correlated with negative health behaviours such as smoking or drinking,[38] poor medication adherence, or lack of disease self-management. There is significant literature that proves that low health literacy leads to more hospitalizations and even higher mortality in the elderly[39]. The definition of health literacy also includes a public health component. This is particularly important as it creates a direct link between individual levels of education and populational health. A review of studies regarding the impact of low literacy on health outcomes highlighted that low literacy resulted in lower preventive measures such as screenings or vaccinations. Recent studies have shown that people with lower health literacy are more reluctant to receive the Covid-19 vaccine, a decision which not only impacts them but also influences the general population[40].

In clinical trials, guidelines from government agencies such as the European Medicines Agency, organizations, and patient advocacy groups request that informed consents and plain language summaries (also called 'lay summaries') for participants are provided in a format that is understandable by a 12-year-old. In literature research conducted by Burks and Keim-Malpass,[41] health literacy assessment tools were used to understand the participant's level of comprehension, perception, and willingness to participate in a clinical trial. It included the Rapid Estimate of Adult Literacy in Medicine (REALM), the Test of Functional Health Literacy in Adults (TOFHLA), and Health Literacy Assessment Using Talking Touchscreen Technology (Health LiTT). The conclusion is that the clinical trial literacy is between that of age 12–18 years old. Simplifying informed consent to improve comprehension is critical for clinical trial participation and reduces any stress that the participants may already face due to their serious diagnosis. It's important that the research process clearly avoids confusion on concepts that include voluntary participation, freedom to withdraw, availability of alternative treatments, unclear survival benefits, unclear risks of adverse events, and potential for receiving placebo.

With the rise of technology, patients have been faced with a new challenge: developing their eHealth literacy. In a paper published in the Journal of Medical Internet Research, Norman and Skinner identified six components to eHealth literacy: traditional literacy and numeracy, computer literacy, information literacy, health literacy, media literacy, and science literacy.[42]

Those working in the digital health space, often take eHealth literacy for granted, assuming that we are all equally knowledgeable in the face of health technologies. But eHealth literacy is a combination of economic, political, cultural, and societal factors.[43] Overall, eHealth literacy is high in developed economies but not with all its citizens. In the European Union, the 2014 European citizens' digital health literacy report[44] showed that 60% of respondents used the Internet to search for health-related questions and 90% of them said that the Internet helped them improve their medical knowledge. Interestingly, 80% of respondents agreed that they knew where to find reliable information, showing a high degree of literacy and maturity in the use of the Internet. These numbers are at odds when considering how many people have low health literacy.

In contrast, studies show a correlation between lower-income individuals and higher health burdens,[45] and the likelihood to have access to healthcare and understandable online health information. Additionally, they are less trusting of health technologies and providers (exacerbating privacy and security risks) and question information provided by the media or the government. Overall, those who need care the most are also those who are less likely to make a meaningful use of technology and information. Given all the positive effects of digital health and patient empowerment discussed in this book, addressing eHealth literacy must become a priority at all levels of healthcare.

Digital solutions have initially been considered a way to reduce the gap in access to health services. Everyone with access to the Internet could also access health services no matter where they were in the world. Telemedicine even promised to offer everyone the same level of access to care and to specialists. However, this approach was based on two false assumptions: that everyone has the same level of digital health literacy and the same level of access to technology. As argued above, there are many inequalities in terms of eHealth literacy. The same is also true when it comes to access to technology.[46] People living in low socioeconomic environments and the elderly have inconsistent access to technology, starting with mobile devices and Internet access. The type of digital solutions available, their interoperability, or the connection speed are not uniform in different geographical areas of the world. Unfortunately, the situation reversed and digital health started creating more disparities than it tried to erase. Inequalities will continue to increase in the upcoming years, with a slice of the population gaining access to better remote care and prevention tools until we address key problems like systemic racism and access issues. In private health systems, where inequalities are already a reality, the gap will only widen creating a health elite with access not only to the best traditional care, but also access to breakthrough digital health services. Public systems based on equal access to care will have to reinvent their model to allow everyone to benefit from the advantages of digital solutions. New healthcare pathways need to be designed, health technologies need to be reimbursed and users need to be educated. The stakes are high as digital solutions hold not only the promise of optimized treatments and medical follow-ups, but also the promise of longer and healthier lives. As technology-based preventive and personalized medicine develops, those with access to digital solutions will be able to better monitor their health, anticipate and prevent diseases, and possibly improve their quality of life. Despite being accessible to most people, the Internet and its ensuing technologies won't benefit all its users. Hence, addressing eHealth literacy in low socioeconomic environments is a key lever to reduce health inequalities, by increasing the use of digital health solutions and promoting patient empowerment.

The Complex World of Health Data

It is impossible to talk about digital innovation and e-patients without ultimately reaching the hot topic of health data. Today, 30% of the world's data is generated by the healthcare industry.[47] Part of these data are generated when users enter in contact information with connected devices. Given the exponential number of wearables (rings, socks, t-shirts, watches, headbands, belts, etc.) and the increasing amount of time spent on our phones and our computers, the volume of data generated will soon reach new highs.

Health data is a complex topic. For some informed experts, it represents a unique opportunity to create a data-driven, effective, and efficient health system, for the benefit of the patient. But for most citizens, health data is just an obscure subject. Occasionally, worrying headlines announce that hospitals have been hacked, medical records have been stolen and sensitive health information has been sold on the dark web. For a subject that already feels wary, this type of negative information only accentuates a feeling of unease.

In the European Union, health data was defined for the first time in the GDPR as

> personal data related to the physical or mental health of a natural person, including the provision of healthcare services, which reveal information about that person's health status.[48]

In the US, HIPAA defined health data as

> individually identifiable information relating to the past, present, or future health status of an individual that is created, collected, or transmitted, or maintained by a HIPAA-covered entity in relation to the provision of healthcare, payment for healthcare services, or use in healthcare operations.[49]

Both definitions are quite broad and encompass most of the data from which it is possible to deduce an individual's health status. This is not only data produced in the context of medical care, but also data generated outside of a health context, using applications or online platforms.

There are many sources of health data, each of which raises new digital security and privacy challenges. These data sources can be divided into two categories:

■ Data from clinical research, the collection, processing, and use of which is subject to a strict framework.
■ Real world data, itself divisible into two categories:
  – Data related to patient care. This is medico-administrative or clinical data collected as part of the health journey.
  – Real-life data generated directly by the patient when browsing online, using connected objects (for example wearables) or applications.

Health data is often described as the new oil: an asset of great value. As such, many companies have heavily invested in this field, collecting raw data, and generating precious insights. This is the case of pharmaceutical companies that rely on health data to assess the efficacy and safety of their drugs and evaluate their use in "real life". It is also the case of healthcare providers such as hospitals whose entire functioning depends on data collection: from allowing doctors to make a diagnosis and define a care plan, to generating reimbursement requests, to managing resources. Hospitals could simply not function if they couldn't access data. Researchers also make use of data to screen for new drug candidates and evaluate new medical procedures. In other words, the entire health system is data dependent. So, what does such a system entail for patients? Does the boom of data-driven use cases represent an opportunity or a threat for users? How can patients benefit from all the value generated by health data?

Notes

1 Sallam HN. Aristotle, godfather of evidence-based medicine. *Facts Views Vis Obgyn*. 2010;2(1):11–19.

2 Wright J. Only your calamity: the beginnings of activism by and for people with AIDS. *Am J Public Health.* 2013;103(10):1788–1798. doi:10.2105/AJPH.2013.301381

3 Sochet A, et al. Health information on the Internet: patient empowerment or patient deceit? *Indian J Med Sci.* 2004;58:321–326.

4 Laugesen J, Hassanein K, Yuan Y. The impact of internet health information on patient compliance: a research model and an empirical study. *J Med Internet Res.* 2015;17:e143.

5 Li HOY, Bailey A, Huynh D, Chan J. YouTube as a source of information on COVID-19: a pandemic of misinformation? *BMJ Glob Health.* 2020;5(5):Article e002604. doi:10.1136/bmjgh-2020-002604

6 Jones AH, Dizon ZB, October TW. Investigation of public perception of brain death using the internet. *Chest.* 2018;154(2):286–292. doi:10.1016/j.chest.2018.01.021

7 Li HOY, Bailey A, Huynh D, Chan J. YouTube as a source of information on COVID-19: a pandemic of misinformation? *BMJ Glob Health.* 2020;5(5):Article e002604. doi:10.1136/bmjgh-2020-002604

8 BBC. Social media firms fail to act on Covid-19 fake news, https://www.bbc.com/news/technology-52903680 (accessed August 2021).

9 TED YouTube channel. Dave deBronkart: Voici Dave, e-patient, www.youtube.com/watch?v=oTxvic-NnAM (accessed August 2021).

10 Kushniruk A. The importance of health information on the internet: how it saved my life and how it can save yours. *J Med Internet Res.* 2019;21(10):e16690. Published 2019 October 27. doi:10.2196/16690

11 Johansson V, Islind AS, Lindroth T, Angenete E, Gellerstedt M. Online communities as a driver for patient empowerment: systematic review. *J Med Internet Res.* 2021 February 9;23(2):e19910. doi:10.2196/19910. PMID: 33560233; PMCID: PMC7902187.

12 Aardoom JJ, Dingemans AE, Boogaard LH, Van Furth EF. Internet and patient empowerment in individuals with symptoms of an eating disorder: a cross-sectional investigation of a pro-recovery focused e-community. *Eat Behav.* 2014 August;15(3):350–356. doi:10.1016/j.eatbeh.2014.04.003. Epub 2014 May 9. PMID: 25064280.

13 Drees J. Google receives more than 1 billion health questions every day, Becker's Health IT, https://www.beckershospitalre-view.com/healthcare-information-technology/google-receives-more-than-1-billion-health-questions-every-day.html (accessed August 2021).

14 Garrity M. Health-related Google searches spike weeks before visiting ER, Becker's Health IT, https://www.beckershospitalre-view.com/patient-experience/health-related-google-searches-spike-weeks-before-visiting-er.html (accessed August 2021).

15 Kantar, The informed digital healthcare consumer, https://www.kantarmedia.com/us/thinking-and-resources/blog/the-informed-digital-healthcare-consumer (accessed August 2021).

16 Bujnowska-Fedak MM, Węgierek P. The impact of online health information on patient health behaviours and making decisions concerning health. *Int J Environ Res Public Health.* 2020;17(3):880. Published 2020 January 31. doi:10.3390/ijerph17030880

17 Weaver JB, Thompson NJ, Weaver SS, Hopkins GL. Healthcare non-adherence decisions and internet health information. *Comput Human Behav.* 2009 November;25(6):1373–1380.

18 Tanis M, Hartmann T, Te Poel F. Online health anxiety and consultation satisfaction: a quantitative exploratory study on their relations. *Patient Educ Couns.* 2016 December;99(7):1227–1232.

19 IAP2 International Federation. IAP2 spectrum of public partici-pation, https://cdn.ymaws.com/www.iap2.org/resource/resmgr/pillars/Spectrum_8.5x11_Print.pdf (accessed August 2021).

20 El Benny M, Kabakian-Khasholian T, El-Jardali F, Bardus M. Application of the eHealth literacy model in digital health interventions: scoping review. *J Med Internet Res.* 2021 June 03;23(6):e23473.

21 Bailo L, Guiddi P, Vergani L, Marton G, Pravettoni G. The patient perspective: investigating patient empowerment enablers and barriers within the oncological care process. *Ecancermedicalscience.* 2019;13:912. Published 2019 March 28. doi:10.3332/ecancer.2019.912

22 Hajat C, Stein E. The global burden of multiple chronic condi-tions: a narrative review. *Prev Med Rep.* 2018;12:284–293. Published 2018 October 19. doi:10.1016/j.pmedr.2018.10.008

23 Holman H, Lorig K. Patient self-management: a key to effectiveness and efficiency in care of chronic disease. *Public Health Rep.* 2004 May–June;119(3):239–243. doi:10.1016/j.phr.2004.04.002. PMID: 15158102; PMCID: PMC1497631.

24 Chatzimarkakis J. Why patients should be more empowered: a European perspective on lessons learned in the management of diabetes. *J Diabetes Sci Technol.* 2010;4(6):1570–1573. Published 2010 November 1. doi:10.1177/193229681000 400634

25 Miaskowski C, Dodd M, West C, et al. Randomized clinical trial of the effectiveness of a self-care intervention to improve cancer pain management. *J Clin Oncol.* 2004;22(9):1713–1720. doi:10.1200/JCO.2004.06.140

26 McCorkle R, Ercolano E, Lazenby M, et al. Self-management: enabling and empowering patients living with cancer as a chronic illness. *CA Cancer J Clin.* 2011;61(1):50–62. doi:10.3322/caac.20093

27 Ferguson T. Online patient-helpers and physicians working together: a new partnership for high quality healthcare. *BMJ.* 2000;321(7269):1129–1132. doi:10.1136/bmj.321.7269.1129

28 Bestsennyy O, Gilbert G, Harris A, Rost J. Telehealth: a quarter-trillion-dollar post-COVID-19 reality? McKinsey & Company, https://www.mckinsey.com/industries/healthcare-systems-and-services/our-insights/telehealth-a-quarter-trillion-dollar-post-covid-19-reality (accessed August 2021).

29 Carter B. Bringing consumer wearables to the next level: preventative healthcare, *Health Tech Hot Spot*, https://health-techhotspot.com/bringing-consumer-wearables-to-the-next-level-preventative-healthcare/ (accessed August 2021).

30 Shapiro E. How an Apple Watch may have saved a teen's life, *abc News*, https://abcnews.go.com/US/apple-watch-saved-teens-life/story?id=33944550 (accessed August 2021).

31 Parasrampuria S, MPH, Henry J, MPH. Hospitals' use of electronic health records data, 2015–2017, The Office of the National Coordinator for Health Information Technology, https://www.healthit.gov/sites/default/files/page/2019-04/AHAEHRUseDataBrief.pdf (accessed August 2021).

32 Open Notes Homepage, https://www.opennotes.org/ (accessed August 2021).

33 Tapuria A, Porat T, Kalra D, Dsouza G, Xiaohui S, Curcin V. Impact of patient access to their electronic health record: systematic review. *Inform Health Soc Care*. 2021 June 2;46(2):192–204. doi:10.1080/17538157.2021.1879810. Epub 2021 Apr 10. PMID: 33840342.

34 Accenture 2019 digital health consumer survey, https://fr.slideshare.net/accenture/accenture-2019-digital-health-consumer-survey (accessed August 2021).

35 Desjardins J. Here are the 50 most important life-saving breakthroughs in history, *Business Insider*, https://www.businessinsider.com/here-are-the-50-most-important-life-saving-breakthroughs-in-history-2018-3 (accessed August 2021).

36 Centers for Disease Control and Prevention. What is health literacy?, https://www.cdc.gov/healthliteracy/learn/index.html (accessed August 2021).

37 Mackert M, Mabry-Flynn A, Champlin S, Donovan EE, Pounders K. Health literacy and health information technology adoption: the potential for a new digital divide. *J Med Internet Res*. 2016;18(10):e264. Published 2016 October 4. doi:10.2196/jmir.6349

38 Zhang F, Or PPL, Chung JWY. How different health literacy dimensions influences health and wellbeing among men and women: the mediating role of health behaviours. *Health Expect*. 2021;24(2):617–627.

39 Berkman ND, Sheridan SL, Donahue KE, Halpern DJ, Crotty K. Low health literacy and health outcomes: an updated systematic review. *Ann Intern Med*. 2011 July 19;155(2):97–107. doi:10.7326/0003-4819-155-2-201107190-00005. PMID: 21768583.

40 Zhang H, Li Y, Peng S, Jiang Y, Jin H, Zhang F. The effect of health literacy on COVID-19 vaccine hesitancy: the moderating role of stress. medRxiv 2021.06.16.21258808; doi:10.1101/2021.06.16.21258808

41 Burks AC, Keim-Malpass J. Health literacy and informed consent for clinical trials: a systematic review and implications for nurses. *Nurs: Res Rev*. 2019;9:31–40 doi:10.2147/NRR.S207497

42 Norman CD, Skinner HA. eHealth literacy: essential skills for consumer health in a networked world. *J Med Internet Res*. 2006;8(2):e9. Published 2006 June 16. doi:10.2196/jmir.8.2.e9

43 Euro Health Net. Digital health literacy: how new skills can help improve health, equity and sustainability, https://euro-healthnet.eu/sites/eurohealthnet.eu/files/publications/PP_Digital%20Health%20Literacy_LR.pdf (accessed August 2021).

44 Directorate-General for the Information Society and Media (European Commission). European citizens' digital health literacy, https://op.europa.eu/en/publication-detail/-/publication/fd42f9e7-937c-41f3-bf03-4221b2db712b (accessed August 2021).

45 Larrimore J. Does a higher income have positive health effects? Using the earned income tax credit to explore the income-health gradient. *Milbank Q*. 2011;89(4):694–727. doi:10.1111/j.1468-0009.2011.00647.x

46 Werts N, Hutton-Rogers L. Barriers to achieving E-health literacy. *Am J Health Sci (AJHS)*. 2013;4(3):115–120. doi:10.19030/ajhs.v4i3.8007

47 Capital Markets. The healthcare data explosion, https://www.rbccm.com/en/gib/healthcare/episode/the_healthcare_data_explosion (accessed August 2021).

48 Privazy Plan. Article 4, EU GDPR, "Definitions", https://www.privacy-regulation.eu/en/article-4-definitions-GDPR.htm (accessed August 2021).

49 Health Information Privacy. Summary of the HIPAA privacy rule, https://www.hhs.gov/hipaa/for-professionals/privacy/laws-regulations/index.html (accessed August 2021).

Chapter 2

From Raw Data to Insights

Before we address the value of patient data or the insights it could create, we need to go back to basics. This is where we use our example of baking a cake. How do we get to the icing of the cake? The cake has many layers and many steps. It has ingredients like flour, sugar, water or in other words our raw material (raw data). Then you need to mix the ingredients (the process), in a blender (system). After you bake the cake (processing/analysis), then you add the filling or icing (reportable). Once the process is complete, do you sell your cake, or give it away for free? How do you make the cake available? What happens if you get feedback on your cake? Do you adjust the ingredients or the process? How about adding carrot to your cake? Although this analogy makes it sound simple, it's not a piece of cake! It's far more complex. Imagine aggregating data from different sources, different organizations with different formats, different standards, de-identified or identifiable data, data privacy, and security. What about the ethics on using data? The revolution of healthcare is in the unlocking of the health data to fuel

DOI:10.4324/9781003215868-2

innovation in research and advance patient care. This chapter will be explaining health data, exploring the value of data when it's curated and consolidated, and how this will empower the patients. Also, we will touch on key questions regarding big data, data strategy, and governance.

Overview of Health Data Types and Sources

In the last few years, we have created so much data, that it accounts approximately 90% of the data in the world. An estimated 2.5 quintillion bytes of data per day. This data comes from everywhere, from social media sites, digital pictures and videos, purchase transaction records, cell phone GPS (global positioning system) signals, and many more.[1] It's expected that by 2025, it's estimated that 463 exabytes ($1,000^6$ bytes) of data will be created each day globally, that's the equivalent of 212,765,957 DVDs per day.[2]

Electronic Health Records: The Main Source of Health Data

After losing her husband to metastatic kidney cancer in 2009, Regina Holliday became an engaged patient advocate. Her cause? Access to electronic health records (EHR) for all patients. Her weapon? Determination.

While her husband was hospitalized, Holliday started asking for his medical records to better understand and research his condition. After spending weeks looking for the precious information, she was told that she would have to wait an additional 21 days to receive the medical record and that it would cost her $0.73 per page. When she was finally able to get her hands on her husband's medical records, she understood the amount of information it contains and how useful it can be if accessible, read and shared with the appropriate professionals. As a result of this experience, she became a well-known patient advocate, fighting for better access to EHR.[3]

Medical records are considered one of the cornerstones of healthcare. They contain all relevant information about a patient: medical history, diagnosis, treatments, allergies, labs tests, imagery, etc. They allow health professionals to treat patients to the best of their abilities, provided that the information contained in EHRs is complete and reliable. In comparison to previous handwritten notes, EHRs represent a significant step forward. They facilitate data accessibility and sharing, decrease the risk for transcription errors and reduce costs associated with repeated medical tests. For physicians, they represent an optimized workflow and time savings.[4]

The global EHR market is expected to grow from $30 billion in 2020 to $40 billion in 2025, driven by technological advances, a need for more centralized medical information, and increased awareness about the importance of digitized medical records.[5] In addition, many governments create incentives for health providers to adopt EHR systems. As an example, in 2009, the US government dedicated $27 billion to incentivize and support EHR implementation across the country. In 2020, adoption rates reached 96% in hospitals and 86% in physician's offices.[6]

Studies report that physicians using EHR systems are more adherent to clinical guidelines and adopt preventive measures such as encouraging influenza and pneumococcal vaccination[7] or prescribing prophylactic care in hospitalized patients with deep vein thrombosis.[8] Reminders and alerts generated by EHRs are also linked to a 55% decrease in serious medication errors in hospitals.[9] Overall, regions with higher EHR adoption have better quality indicators and lower costs than their counterparts.[10] EHRs also played a critical role in detecting and fighting the Covid-19 pandemic. Data poured into medical records was used to identify risk factors, monitor for disease complications, feed artificial intelligence algorithms to predict and prevent negative outcomes, support clinical decision-making, or inform biomedical research.[11]

While medical records were initially only destined to health providers, patients are increasingly gaining access to this information as well. Approximately 75% of studies assessing the impact of access to medical records on patients found it brought benefits, going from simple reassurance to positive medical outcomes.[12] The list of advantages is very long: patients with access to their medical records were found to be better informed and engaged in their care, less anxious, and more trusting of their medical team. Moreover, patients are also able to contribute to their medical records by signalling any errors or missing information. Medical errors caused by inaccurate EHR data are sometimes reported. In 2008, a patient suffering from kidney cancer had his only healthy kidney removed because the EHR identified the wrong organ as cancerous.[13] Finally, although some physicians worried about the disclosure of sensitive medical information and considered that patients should not necessary be aware of all their medical data,[14] studies show that in practice, it brings no significant negative consequences.[15]

Patients are increasingly encouraged to seek access to their medical records and many health facilities and governments create patient portals. In the US the "Get it. Check it. Use it." campaign was designed to inform patients about their rights regarding their EHRs and encourage them to review their information to make sure that it contains no mistakes. The Blue Button logo was developed to inform patients that they can safely download their medical data from the platform they are using. Despite these efforts, a 2019 study showed that only 10% of patients with access to their medical records made use of it.[16] Among the reasons often invoked is that in practice, the road to EHR access is paved with high fees, delays, and inefficient processes.[17] In countries where EHRs are not as widespread and patients are less informed about their rights regarding EHR access (if they even exist!), the situation can be even worse.

In contrast, private tech companies are developing apps that allow patients to aggregate data from multiple sources and even fill in their medical history. The facility with which these apps collect information and provide insights and analytics is baffling when compared to the complexity of achieving these same tasks in the regular health system. Driven by the development and adoption of interoperability standards such as FHIR (discussed further on) and growing public demand, the tech giants are entering the EHR space and deciding to make waves. For example, companies such as Apple added a Health Records section to the Health app, which allows patients to aggregate all their medical records in one accessible place.[18]

Medical Data Is Not Sufficient to Understand the Human behind the Patient

When considering the regulatory definitions of health data presented in Chapter 1, health data cannot be resumed to the clinical and administrative information contained in EHRs. Approximately 89% of care occurs outside of a medical setting, therefore, not captured by EHRs. Indeed, when considering the determinants of health, medical care only represents 11%. The rest is made of the environment (7%), individual behaviour (36%), social circumstances (24%), genetics and biology (22%).

Other data outside of medical care setting are:

- Environment: refers to the place we live in and includes parameters such as air and water quality, exposure to loud noise, toxic elements or allergens, or the access we have to recreational activity, transportation, jobs, and safety. This determinant is often tracked by governmental institutions that measure these parameters and usually render this data public;

- Individual behaviour: is the largest determinant of health, refers to our habits such as smoking, drinking, sleeping, exercising, nutrition, exposure to stress factors, or high-risk behaviour. These habits can also be quantified through wearables that measure our physical activity and sleeping patterns, or apps that keep track of our other activities;
- Social circumstances: refer to the social environment we grew up and lived in. Our gender, social status, culture, traditions, work conditions, ethnicity, etc. all have an impact on our health outcomes and quality-of-life; and
- Genetics and biology: refer to genes and physiology. This will become more and more important in upcoming years as genome sequencing technique will become more accessible and commonly used. They will allow patients to better understand their current health and anticipate potential evolutions. They can be measured through regular lab tests and imagery, but they can also be tracked through wearables, at-home medical test devices or apps.

Each of these health determinants can be measured to some extent. Access to all this information, called "big data", can create a very precise vision of an individual and allow medical professionals to better treat their patients.

What Is Big Data and Where Does All This Data Come From?

All this data comes from various sources. The most well-known is clinical data extracted from EHR. It holds the advantage of being available in real-time and provides a quite comprehensive vision of a patient's medical journey and health status. But EHR data only accounts for a small percentage of data available in healthcare. Other sources include national databases, clinical research databases, administrative databases, registries and cohorts, patient-generated data sources (e.g. wearables, social media), and other privately held health databases.

National databases contain very large datasets that inform about the population's health. They are used in research, but they can also be used to manage the health system, as it has been the case during the Covid-19 pandemic. These databases can either be available in open access, meaning that users can freely download and analyze data online, or require an access permission. Depending on the country, procedures to access the data can be quite long and expensive. The quality of data stored in these databases can vary but they provide the advantage of being very complete and give a rapid overview of population-related health questions.

Clinical research databases contain data produced during a clinical trial either by a private or a public organization. Data quality is usually high because information is collected in a standardized format through purpose-built software. The inconvenience is that data produced during a clinical trial is often impossible to use in another setting, as it was collected with a precise scope. Some organizations are looking into the possible reuse of clinical trial data for other research with the permission of patients. By reusing high quality data instead of going through the entire collection process again, some studies could be accelerated.

Administrative databases or claims databases are usually used for billing purposes. In most technologically advanced countries, medical information is coded, meaning that each procedure or treatment is recorded as a code. This system allows for standardized and uniformized databases that are easier to work with. However, as they are designed for administrative purposes, they provide little clinical insights into a patient or a population.

Cohorts and registries are databases designed to capture information on a target population, usually focused on a feature such as a disease or a treatment. One of the largest cohorts in the world is held by American company 23andme, specialized in genome sequencing. It contains the genotypic and the phenotypic data of over 6 million people. Other examples include the China PEACE (Patient-centred Evaluative Assessment of Cardiac Events) Million Persons Project, a cohort of 2 million citizens aimed at identifying cardiovascular risk factors, or the Million Women Study in the UK designed to assess the risk of breast cancer in women using hormone replacement therapy after menopause. Globally, the number of cohorts has been increasing since the 90s, driven by a growing interest in real-world data versus traditional data extracted from clinical trials. Over one-third of the largest international cohorts collect genetic data, a number that has been increasing in recent years due to the decreasing cost of genome sequencing.

What Are the Key Steps in the Data Value Chain?

What Is Raw Data?

Raw data is the unprocessed data (computer- or paper-based) that is captured, filed, and stored. Raw data is also seen as the source data, where data was first captured or documented. For example, doctor's notes, laboratory data collected before interpretation, or a measurement of blood pressure in a device before algorithm or analysis of the data.

What Is Value Data?

Value data is the true power of data when put into context, it creates insights and provides information that will allow a person or an organization to be better informed and make data-driven decisions. Figure 2.1 shows the steps from raw data to value data. Starting from the concept to identifying what information and data is needed, how data will be collected to be processed, made accessible via for example data warehouse for analysis using business intelligence tools (reporting but could also include machine learning), and then come full circle to be reused or repurposed. In addition, the important step is archiving the data, in order words, housekeeping and record keeping. When we talk about value data, we refer to data that has been processed and it's ready to be used for analysis. The process is a cycle when data is reused to support a different or new use case. It makes it easier for organizations to reuse and repurpose as the processing of the data includes from cleaning the data (such as removing outliers) to applying the standards (using for example same format each time) and following the FAIR and TRUST principles which will be described later in this chapter. This process is extremely time-consuming and costly for organizations managing huge volumes of data. Therefore, repurposing and reusing is usually the preferred option.

Combining value data and analytics, creates deep insights that can enable smarter decisions, optimize strategies, and in case of patients, make better decisions about their health. Deep

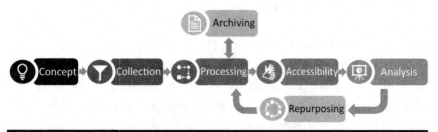

Figure 2.1   From raw to value data.

insights are basically gaining a deep understanding of a complex situation. For example, a male patient visited his doctor as he was not feeling well. He had chest pain, headaches, difficulty in breathing, blurred vision, and fatigue. The doctor asked about family history and decided to take his vital signs, including blood pressure. His systolic pressure was over 140 mm Hg and diastolic of over 90 mm Hg. These are all raw data collected by the doctor either using his notes or devices. His blood pressure was over normal ranges, indication of hypertension. The doctor decided to do further tests, including urine and blood test for level of cholesterol. It's through a combination of raw data collected by the doctor, devices, and lab test and results, that the doctor was able to diagnose the patient as having hypertension (deep insights). With this information, the doctor can prescribe the right medication and also recommend changes to the patient's lifestyle. All the pieces of data and the combination of those such as the ranges for high and low blood pressure, symptoms, medical history including family medical history, and lab results to provide the deep insight to generate the information (contextualize) to a diagnosis.

Most health data is produced by the patients themselves through their daily activities. It can be using a smart object, posting a message on social media, or accessing a Wikipedia page. This data is particularly important because it can help prevent diseases, anticipate outbreaks, or detect early side effects from a treatment way before an individual enters the traditional health systems and provides data for official control bodies. As an example, a group of Italian researchers published a study showing that early-warning signs of Covid-19 were available on Twitter way before the first official reports of local cases emerged. The researchers focused specifically on the number of posts mentioning the word "pneumonia" which drastically increased starting in December of 2019, way before any cases were announced by health authorities.[19] Companies such as Kap Code analyzed social media posts to identify public responses to fake news, the state of mental health in young adults or the effect of the pandemic on the population. Similarly, a pregnancy can be detected based on the online purchases of an expecting mother or the Facebook groups she joins. A suicide attempt can be anticipated based on Google searches, the content of social media posts or the activity levels captured by wearables. Without even knowing, users leave breadcrumbs of health information almost everywhere they go. But patients can also actively generate information to speed up or improve their care. Talking to Dave deBronkart, he mentioned the story of Kristina Sheridan and her daughter Kate. Kate contracted Lyme disease after a grammar camp. Slowly, her condition started to deteriorate, taking away all her energy and academic capacities. She could not read, write, or run anymore. Her symptoms became so overwhelming that she didn't know what to tell doctors anymore. It became impossible for her to explain every detail of her medical records each time she saw a new doctor because of the amount of overlapping information it contained. Her mother Kristina decided to write all the symptoms on an Excel spreadsheet to help her daughter to keep track of her health, and to be able to tell her medical story more effectively. Having all this data empowered her to better communicate with her medical team but also have a more holistic view of her health. As a result, she was able to improve both her physical and mental health. Patient-generated data doesn't just provide medical information, it also provides a snippet into a person's life. A bad lab result might result in a child missing their birthday because of an emergency hospitalization, an improvement in a condition can represent a way out of a depression. Behind lab test values lie humans whose whole lives depend on those numbers. Failing to capture the patient's own experience, through patient-generated data, is reducing an individual to numbers.

We are living in a world of 'Digital Data Wild West'. Many organizations are struggling to figure out how to harness and unlock the value of mountains of data they are sitting on.

Data needs to be looked at multi-dimensionally to understand the true value that can turn raw data into insights. Data is the "new oil". How do we refine it, how do we purpose it, and how do we reuse it?

Firstly, we need to acknowledge that every data has value. Some might say the opposite or that value comes with the purpose. We need to acquire the data, to prepare and classify the data, filter out noise to derive the value. It is important to understand what the data tells us (information), what insights might provide with analytics, and make it actionable.

We need to address the data:

- Availability: where is the data, how to access, connected.
- Usability: format, language, metadata.
- Integrity: data files not corrupted, code changes.
- Security: safe from accidental changes, future proof.

The data can be used for descriptive, diagnostic, predictive, and prescriptive analytics.

Descriptive
Standard reporting that provides information about what already has happened

Diagnostic
Mines data to understand why something happened

Predictive
Using statistical models and algorithms to be able to predict outcomes based on previous actions

Prescriptive
Cutting edge of data analytics to prescribe and to define the best course of future action

MINI CASE STUDY 2.1: APPLE'S CONSUMER HEALTH AND WELLNESS APP

As part of the Apple's consumer health and wellness, they have built new innovative health features giving the users the ability to securely share their data with their caregivers, family, and health practitioners. In addition, their new iOS 15 can be used to measure and identify a person's health data. It also provides trend analysis for 20 types of data ranging from resting heart rate to sleep to cardio fitness.[20]

Data sharing is one of the key components that would be crucial in the journey for patient empowerment. Granting the full control over which data they can share and with whom they want to share it with. This is the beginning of building a personalized patient's health ecosystem. With this enhancement from Apple, what is the strategy going forward? We understand the benefits for patients but how does this benefit Apple? How do they use the data collected?

If additional enhancements could be added, such as integrating with various IoT devices, embed laboratory results, and genomics data in an aggregated way, it could provide trends, and compare it to other device users, or even better the population based on healthcare data and demographic data. This will give a full picture of not only the person's complete health information and to decide on the right treatment of care or improve quality of life but also providing a good overview of the population and where healthcare systems might need to focus on or improve on. Also potentially used the information for early diagnosis and prevention powered by AI.

How do we manage data ownership from various devices and data sources? The data is heterogeneous, levels of control and security varies per provider, the level of data accuracy might also be different between wearables, and what if you have different wearables tracking same vital signs, how to manage the disparities and conflicting data that might give false negatives or positives?

We need to understand that not all devices and apps are classified as medical devices. We are still at the early stages of defining what that baseline for measuring or assessing health is when using wearables, sensors, or devices compare with the current approved methods. Medical devices go through regulatory qualification and certification before they can be used for the intended population (e.g. adults, paediatrics) and approved for the intended use. If the apps or devices are not of medical grade, it might not meet the requirements set by the health authorities regarding safety, effectiveness, data privacy, and security.

Companies that have a digital strategy, do not necessarily have a data strategy. This could present a problem if the organizations have many systems which use different platforms, manage different datasets, lack data prioritization, definitions, standards, measurements, etc. The data strategy helps organizations to be data-driven decision-making companies, enhancing their processes, and making it more efficient. It also needs to align with business strategy on data needs. They need to have a strategic plan to be able to collect all relevant data that can drive business outcomes. Also, it needs to be a company wide data policy that covers all different types of data sources including critical data from how data is captured, stored, and managed. It's important to have a data governance framework to establish policies, standards, compliance, security, data integrity, master data management, and resources to support operations, architecture, and change management. In addition, helps to focus data efforts where it creates not only the most value but a long-term value for the organization. Implementing a data culture within the organization to be analytics-driven enabled data intelligence. Organizations also must understand that this is an ongoing process that must be continuously reviewed and enhanced to align with ongoing needs and have a mindset of outside-in approach on the most advanced solutions and changing market to inform their strategy.

Overall, this will help organizations to be information literate and make better decision in the future using the data to analyse their own operations, performance, data mining, etc.

Big technology companies like Amazon offers its AWS product in a way that provides infrastructure as a service (IaaS) on a subscription basis. With the increase of digital connectivity and internet use, there has been a surge of data that can potentially provide value not just to companies but to society in general. There are many companies exploring innovative ways to unlock the value of data and embedding trust, privacy, and security into their models. Therefore, becoming 'digital at the core' can potentially create more sustainable value especially for healthcare systems and organizations to create a more data-driven organization that will benefit patients and improve their care. Also, enhancing their processes, thereby, making it more efficient.

Who Are the Key Players?

There are various key players in the health data value chain. The key players are the patients, government, insurance companies, hospitals, pharmaceutical companies, academia, clinical research organizations, and big technology corporations.

The actors can be categorized in the following:

1. **Patients:** person who receives or is registered to receive medical care or treatment.
2. **Patient Advocacy Groups:** organized non-profit groups support people and their families that are affected by a specific medical condition.

3. **Health Providers:** organizations or individuals that provide care to patients (e.g. hospitals, clinics, physicians, pharmacists, radiologists).
4. **Payers:** organizations or individuals that pay providers for the health services (e.g. insurance companies, government).
5. **Researchers:** organizations that conduct research or clinical studies (e.g. pharmaceutical companies, academia, and others).
6. **Health Agencies:** government bodies that approve medicines, devices, and procedures. They also protect and promotes health, wellbeing, and safety of their citizens.
7. **Vendors:** organizations that sell medical devices, pharmaceutical products, services and solutions (e.g. technology companies including devices, clinical research organizations, and data brokers).

All actors can be data producers and consumers. But without patients that initiates that data generation, there wouldn't be any health data that could be collected, used, and shared. As we stated in Chapter 1, patients are at the top of the pinnacle. Patients are the number one stakeholder, as they have more at stake.

Data is used for different purposes. Defining the purpose is key to understanding who needs access, what type of access is needed, who can control the data, what type of securities and measures need to be in place, would the data be shared and exported, etc. Having a map of the different actors will help to prioritize key players and understand their needs, whether it is to improve their health and wellbeing, for the greater good or society, for research, for commercial purposes, or other.

Where Do the Patients Come In?

Preferably at the beginning, as a partner. The fact is that patients are sitting at one end of the value chain and have no visibility over the rest. There needs to be transparency on how their data has been used, transformed, reused, stored, managed, reported, and the key aspect is 'what's in it for them and society'.

It is important to partner with patients through the continuum of the health ecosystem. There needs to be a shift of mindset starting with patients are not 'subjects' and referred to as a third person.

In discussion with Deborah Collyar, she said:

> health literacy principles need to apply for any medical information, including visual, numerically. What's always missing for patients is context. What's the landscape and how this info fits in to what they need and their experience e.g. daily life. There needs to be accuracy, coordination, and have an approach that all elements come together to support the patients and families especially through their experience and journey. There needs to be a share decision-making, patients need to be involved. There has to be a right type of communication and multi-logue (dialogue). Where decisions are made, full access of information (to be made available and in plain language). Patients should still have the option for the medical team to make the decision for them.

If we involve patients from the beginning, it's already a good start. It is important to include the patient's voice, especially when relevant symptoms are not catalogued by science. "It is an inversion of who knows relevant information", said Dave deBronkart.

> Good things will happen when data gets liberated. It will take decades before it evolves to be newly enabled. In an ideal system, there is a steady supply

of information about people's health and have the autonomy to take care of "my business", and "my records".

Input from Patient advisory boards (PABs) has become a common practice in many pharmaceutical companies especially in clinical research to support protocol design, clinical trial execution, design of informed consent form, clinical trial medicine kit design, wearable devices and mobile applications, and patient-communication materials. PAB provides the patients' voices and the opportunity to learn about other patients' personal journeys. The non-profit organization, Center for Information and Study on Clinical Research Participation (CISCRP) has been facilitating PABs on behalf of clinical teams and research sponsors in both public- and private-sector organizations. Additionally, regulatory agencies in Europe and North America have been involving patient communities for input. For example, the US Food and Drug Administration has been holding meetings among patients and advocacy groups with select rare diseases (such as Fabry) as part of its Patient-Focused Drug Development initiative and its Patient Engagement Advisory Committee. The purposes of the Patient-Focused Drug Development initiative are to hear directly from patients with rare medical conditions to better understand how these illnesses are being managed and to identify beneficial outcomes that should be targeted by investigational drugs and biologics.[21]

What Are Some of the Challenges of This Value Chain?

We define and group the critical challenges that we foresee in the patient data value chain. There is no bulletproof type of solution or infrastructure but it's important to understand the potential risks not only for the organization but the data they either own or manage. Hence, the repercussions if no safeguard is put in place, it could damage the company's reputation let alone the damage caused at the social and individual level.

#1 Trust

Putting patients and individuals at the centre is so important. Trust is the foundation. It's the trust of organizations and how they manage our data privately and securely (cybersecurity) that can make the difference. Also understanding the intent of data collection or acquisition. Trust depends on the geography. Sabina Kineen, a patient, caregiver, patient advocate for Fabry Disease, and FDA guest speaker for the Patient-Focused Drug Development said,

> there will be pushback from people who are weary of technology. Also, the political situation in US has led to misinformation and distrust, many people have pulled back, weary that someone is looking at their data without them knowing. But then you have a generation that trust everything digital. As opposed to many in the older generation who may lack awareness or education in technology. In addition, the disparity across different cultures, people of varying socio-economic statuses, rural vs. urban environments…all of these things make it even more challenging.

#2 Inequalities

Data inequalities are related to the 'data divide' that digitalization has created. This is bigger than who has access to digital solutions and Internet. This is the social-economic divide, rural vs. urban, and the diversity of the data that is collected from citizens. This gap affects the development of more complex data analytics like machine learning and artificial intelligence, representing only parts of the population that are not fit for purpose and giving an improper representation of the reality.

#3 Heterogeneous and Multi-Dimensional

Managing huge quantities of data that are unstructured and might come in different formats and standards from documents, videos, audio, text files, and other sources. Heterogeneous features provide different types of representations for the same individuals. It might be difficult to integrate heterogeneous data to meet business needs due to a variety of data acquisition including historical data and metadata (e.g. geographic location, timestamp).

#4 Autonomous Sources with Distrusted Control

Data comes from different sources and organizations. Autonomous is the ability of each data source to generate and collect information but the issue is with distrusted control or no centralized control and data governance framework. It questions the source of the data and whether all the data were captured with e.g. the right level of consent, level of accuracy, data cleaning process, mapping, and use of standards.

#5 Complex and Evolving Relationship

With the exponential increase on the volume of data, the complexity and the correlations among them increases. From the acquisition, cleaning, integration to linking of the data.

This is especially crucial for predictive and prescriptive analytics.

#6 Skilled People

The lack of skilled people to handle big data. It ranges from data engineer, data analysts, data scientists but also technologists, developers, standard curators, and others. It's a combination of different roles and having the right data governance to fulfil the needs of the organization. Also consider resources required to scale up the solutions including change management.

Addressing the Obstacles of Big Data in Healthcare

Although health data comes with many benefits for the entire health system, it also creates many challenges that need to be tackled in the upcoming years. First of all, there is an increasing number of data sources that pose problems in terms of:

Storage

When discussing raw and value data, we also need to address the challenges of big data as discussed earlier. For example, when using a device (Internet of Things) that continuously collects heart rate, temperature, and movement, the amount of data captured increases exponentially (terabytes) and the need for big data storage. When you use multiple devices, different systems that collect your medical information, laboratory results, imaging, or scans, etc. the complexity increases. Big data is where the 6 Vs become very important: Volume, Velocity, Variety, Variability, Veracity, and Value (Figure 2.2).[22]

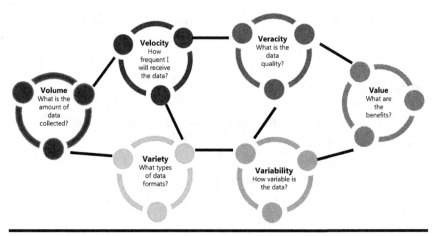

Figure 2.2 The 6 Vs of big data.

Governance

The second challenge that emerges with health data is governance. Where, who, and how the data is managed? As any system, there is a need for data strategy and governance. Also, a structure around the management of systems that stores the data. But what is the flaw in data governance? The governance should include all stakeholders, unfortunately, patients rarely have a seat on the table. In Chapter 3, we will describe the different roles in health data and propose the different stakeholders to collaborate and co-create "the ideal" governance system.

Interoperability

The more you listen to stories about patients taking control over their data to improve their care, the more you realize that 90% of those stories have a common element: patients complain about the lack of interoperability of various data sources. Health interoperability is defined by HIMSS (Healthcare Information and Management Systems Society), a non-profit organization, as "the ability of different information systems, devices and applications (systems) to access, exchange, integrate and cooperatively use data in a coordinated manner, within and across organizational, regional, and national boundaries."[23] It is well known by now, in the healthcare industry, data lies in big silos. This creates a paradox since health providers need real-time access to a variety of data sources to provide good quality care, yet, because health data is so sensitive and valuable, there are many barriers to access. The lack of interoperability in healthcare constrains some physicians to diagnose and treat patients with partial information. It is like driving a car on the highway with one eye closed. To compensate for the missing information, providers take a lot of time and resources to piece together a patient's medical history and order complementary tests that might already exist elsewhere. This automatically leads to poorer outcomes and greater costs.

According to a 2018 HIMSS research, US hospitals have an average of 16 different EHR vendors. Of course, that includes specialty EHR, but it still translates a large number of different systems that, depending on the vendor, might not communicate with one another. Initially, the American strategy was to equip all health providers with EHR systems and encourage their meaningful use. However, they soon realized that by doing so, they were spreading data across multiple systems that didn't talk to each other and provided fragments or a patient's entire journey. So, the priorities started to shift, and interoperability became a key focus.[24] This move is accentuated by consumer demand emerging from services like Apple Health that are automatically interoperable with a vast majority of other health apps and connected objects, creating an easy to access data repository about an individual's entire health.

One way of addressing interoperability challenges is using standards that provide a common language and set of rules for systems to send and receive information from one another.

Recently, the Fast Healthcare Interoperability Resource (FHIR) has been gaining traction as a way of connecting disparate healthcare information systems. Many countries have developed regulatory frameworks or incentives to encourage vendors to develop interoperable systems and health providers to adopt them.

Security and Privacy

With digitalization, we have seen the increase of security breaches. These new threats have not been anticipated with conventional cyber security systems. The reason is many systems are not designed with the level of security in mind. Therefore, hackable by design. Unfortunately, this is the reality that we live in today.

The current generation of heavy internet users are creating masses of information on the web, they are digital denizens. They are also creating a "digital exhaust" not only via the web but also via Internet of Things (IoT). Third parties can create rich identities out of these data deposits, to use and abuse as they see fit. Therefore, authentication must be a key component in the design of systems to have the ability to clearly identify and trust both digital and physical data sources in order to develop a reliable system.

The rise of digital solutions that lack the right security levels are creating an unprecedented potential security breach. The same interconnectivity that can create value also can be compromised. This could trigger political, social, and economic effects. The problem is that not all security challenges are obvious.

Data privacy has been playing an increasing role in the public debate. In May 2018, the European Union implemented the EU General Data Protection Regulation (GDPR) to define clear roles and responsibilities in the collection and processing of personal data. Despite this and similar other initiatives across the globe, many concerns still exist, fuelled by scandals such as Cambridge Analytics or suspicions of data misuse by other big tech companies.

There is no doubt that the discussion around data privacy will become paramount in the next couple of years both for citizens and lawmakers. In parallel, the number of health data initiatives will skyrocket, driven by considerable investments in this field. In the past couple of years alone, big tech companies like Amazon, Apple, and Google have made a giant step into healthcare. Whether it is through direct-to-consumer devices and services or business-oriented data storage and analytics capabilities, many companies have entered the health market. But many announcements left the general public with a feeling of unease: software provider Epic announced an initiative to compile de-identified data from 20 million citizens to accelerate research, the NHS signed partnerships Amazon to provide access to millions of medical records, and Google acquired wearables brand FitBit and its rich health database.

In parallel, the number of data breaches has exploded. According to HIPAA Journal,[25] between 2009 and 2020, 3,705 healthcare data breaches have been reported to the Department of Health and Human Services Office for Civil Rights. Those breaches have resulted in the loss, theft, exposure, or impermissible disclosure of over 268 million healthcare records, more than 81% of the population of the United States.

Data privacy is important to protect individuals using a service or solution to trust organizations to handle their personal data with care. The purpose is controlling the access especially to sensitive data.

Some examples of data privacy laws are:

1. Data Protection Act (UK): controls how your personal information is used by organizations, businesses, or the

government. Everyone responsible for using personal data has to follow strict rules called 'data protection principles'. They must make sure the information is:
- used fairly, lawfully, and transparently
- used for specified, explicit purposes
- used in a way that is adequate, relevant, and limited to only what is necessary
- accurate and, where necessary, kept up to date
- kept for no longer than is necessary
- handled in a way that ensures appropriate security, including protection against unlawful or unauthorized processing, access, loss, destruction or damage[26]

2. HIPAA (Health Insurance Portability and Accountability Act of 1996) US: a federal law that required the creation of national standards to protect sensitive patient health information from being disclosed without the patient's consent or knowledge. It gives its citizens rights over their health information.[27]

3. The European Union's GDPR: requires organizations to safeguard personal data and uphold the privacy rights of anyone in EU territory. The regulation includes seven principles of data protection that must be implemented and eight privacy rights that must be facilitated. It also empowers member state-level data protection authorities to enforce the GDPR with sanctions and fines. It went into effect in 2018.[28]

However, users still struggle to balance consent with how their data would be used. This is partly because of unanswered questions on the intent, policy, and procedures related to personal identifiable data.

Potential way to address personal data protection requirements, and an approved legal basis for data processing, is to anonymize the data whilst maintaining sufficient information to conduct scientific research. But data anonymization can never be 100% absolute. There is always a residual risk of patient identification which is more likely in a big data context as data are triangulated with other datasets of which the data sharer might be unaware of. Even if data generation might be a single or multiregional, data sharing is likely to be global. As individual data increases, the population level uniqueness also increases. Data Protection Authorities have also argued that data anonymization must be re-evaluated over time as the data environment changes. This challenges the technical and legal adequacy of a release-and-forget anonymization model and speaks to a need that re-identification risks should be reassessed regularly.[29]

However, it is important to understand that these scandals are only the visible part of the iceberg. The part that is constantly covered in the media and that creates fear and doubts. As a matter of fact, citizens instinctively understand that their health information is more sensitive that other types of data. A 2018 DRG report showed that 45% of EU5 (France, UK, Germany, Italy and Spain) consumers were more concerned with the privacy of their health records than that of other types of data. But health data cannot be resumed to privacy and security concerns. We believe it is safe to say that data is the fuel of the entire health system, without it, nothing would no longer work.

The question is: How do we make the data accessible, reliable, and secure?

Where Does Ethics Play a Key Part?

We remember when GDPR was being rolled out in the EU. Organizations were striving to meet the requirements and decipher what "right to be forgotten" means. Could you be forgotten in the healthcare system or clear your criminal records if you have one? Where is the balance? We recall a comical rumour that GDPR was put in place to stop getting too many junk emails. We wish that was true. Even with GDPR, we don't recall consenting to getting junk emails, but we still do. For organization to sell our data without us benefiting in any way, where is the ethics in all this? If we truly exercise our "rights to be forgotten" in the healthcare system, isn't that unethical. In a pandemic situation, if we would not be able to track and trace, contain the pandemic, and the government is not able to provide the right level of healthcare, how ethical would that be?

Another ethics issue we have come across many times and surely everyone does, is who reads the fine prints on consent forms or the terms and conditions? It is unusual for a user to actually read a website's terms of use, and then carefully set their privacy controls. There are almost never repercussions for organizations that fail to abide by their terms of use, or that negligently leak information. If a person has no understanding of what they are consenting, clearly, it's pure manipulation for people to agree to hand over their data as like handing over their credit card details with their pin code. Organizations have to be transparent and do better in explaining how the person's data would be used, for what purpose is shared, and to be notified when changes occur. This is the way to earn the people's trust back. Also be able to police themselves when there is a misuse of information that has no benefit to the individual or even worse mismanagement of data. It's not rocket science, it's about decency. If we do something for you, you do something in return, quid pro quo. For companies who still have the indecency to justify "we had a data breach, but the data is anonymized and there is no way to identify you", that is beside the point. We place our trust in you and you mishandled it and did not fully disclose the consequences. This is another reason why patient empowerment must tackle ethical issues of misuse and mishandling of data. Also creating more awareness and training to reduce this risk.

Floridi and Taddeo[30] consider data ethics as a new branch of ethics which:

> studies and evaluates moral problems related to data (including generation, recording, curation, processing, dissemination, sharing, and use), algorithms (including AI, artificial agents, machine learning, and robots), and corresponding practices (including responsible innovation, programming, hacking, and professional codes), in order to formulate and support morally good solutions (e.g. right conducts or right values).

Key issues are possible re-identification of individuals through data mining, linking, merging, and reusing of large datasets. Also, a crucial topic is data ownership (as described in Chapter 3). Especially more so as data is being commercialized for big data use and anonymized data that removes the need to request additional consent from users or participants in research. These challenges are not just ethical but also connected to legal and data privacy concerns.

Open Data, FAIR, and TRUST Principles

You might have heard about open data, maybe not so much about FAIR (Findable Accessible Interoperable Reusable) data. Open data is data that can be used freely, modify, and share for any purpose as long as it preserves provenance (origin of where it came from) and openness.[31]

Open data is publicly accessible. It is data that can be accessed, used, and shared by anyone and for any purpose. Therefore, the data must be anonymized and not contain any information that might identify any one individual.

For example, NHS (UK's National Health System) uses open data as it brings huge opportunities to:

- Increase patient choice.
- Improving patient outcomes.
- Creating increased productivity.
- Contributing to economic growth.

FAIR principle highlights the need to embrace good practice by defining essential characteristics of data objects to ensure that data are reusable. If FAIR principles were not applied, it would be very costly to maintain, difficult to integrate data, and very likely for the system to remain siloed. The benefits of implementing FAIR principles results in various improvements including possibilities for robotics and process automation. FAIR data saves time especially the data scientist in cleaning, transforming, and aggregating large scale data sources. It allows to manage and reuse data also to increase the transparency, improves discoverability, and reusability of digital data.

Maintaining data FAIR requires trustworthy digital repositories (TDRs) with sustainable governance, best practices or policies, and reliable infrastructure. This will increase the trust of users on the data stewards and custodians, as described later in Chapter 3. According to Lin D. et al, TDRs must enable access and reuse of data over time for the communities or users they serve and establishing the accepted criteria of the data that will be surfaced. In addition, to support data curation and preservation of data that holds different levels of reusability for example the patient's email address might be used as a username to log in to their EHR or used to contact the patient. TDR also needs to communicate the level of data quality, for example if the email address has been confirmed by the patient and frequency of review or confirmation.[32]

In order to realize FAIR data stewardship especially in research we need to respect citizen's rights related to privacy and confidentiality. Also, a governance framework capable of fostering trust and participation.[33]

The data revolution creates endless opportunities to tackle different challenges. As data is proliferating at an unprecedented pace so must our ability to analyse and contextualize it. Drawing genuine insights from data will require the right skillset. Also, putting insights into action requires a careful understanding of the potential ethical consequences not only for individuals but also for organizations. In discussion with Angus Gunn from Center for Medical Technology Policy (CMTP), he stresses that when collecting big data, we need to understand how we use it, and for what purpose. The reality is that Real World Data (RWD) is highly heterogeneous and varies per country per state, and it's unstructured. How do we interrogate that? The answer is that we need a methodology. Ideally, a harmonized approach on data collection for patients using a universal platform where all the outcomes are captured including disease history, using ICD-10-CM (described in the subsequent section), free text that is informative and could be interrogated in a uniform way for supportive or investigative purposes.

With all the data collected, it becomes a big responsibility of how we need to manage it. We need to ensure that it follows the TRUST Principles of data repositories (Table 2.1, Lin D. et al.). Transparency, Responsibility, User focus, Sustainability and Technology: the TRUST Principles provide a common framework to facilitate discussion and implementation of best practice in digital preservation by all stakeholders. This is important especially for data stewardship to provide trustworthiness of the data by demonstrating through evidence that the repositories ensure data integrity, authenticity, accuracy, reliability, and accessibility over extended time frames. These repositories require regular audits and certification.

Table 2.1 TRUST Principles for Digital Repositories

Principle	Guidance for Repositories
Transparency	To be transparent about specific repository services and data holdings that are verifiable by publicly accessible evidence.
Responsibility	To be responsible for ensuring the authenticity and integrity of data holdings and for the reliability and persistence of its service.
User Focus	To ensure that the data management norms and expectations of target user communities are met.
Sustainability	To sustain services and preserve data holdings for the long-term.
Technology	To provide infrastructure and capabilities to support secure, persistent, and reliable services.

Would TRUST on FAIR enable patient empowerment? How do we enable citizen's participation and data sharing? We need to have trust in the system that controls and manages our data. We need to understand what type of permissions are asked and granted, how our data is being used and for what purposes, how do you govern ethically the use of data? The problem is that our data is already accessible, publicly whether we like it or not, whether we granted permission or not. Even for data granted with consent, the terms and conditions are too vague, without purpose, without naming its affiliates and partners, and too technical for an ordinary person to understand. It is a systemic problem. Even if an organization has its best intents, there have been too many actors that have corrupted or manipulated the system which makes us wary of sharing our data freely. Until we don't have trust in the system and trust on how data is being handled, adoption might take years. We need to start from somewhere, awareness and education for citizens like us but organizations and big corporations also need to be educated even more on how they disseminate information and start treating people as human beings beyond the data.

What Is the Right Type of Data Governance?

Data governance is a framework that helps organizations identify and meet their information needs involving different data stakeholders, defining the standards, processes, and procedures to manage the data (including metadata).

The evolution of digital solutions, especially the IoT has led to decentralized systems that lack proper governance and operate as silos. In order for IoT to realize its potential, these fragmented systems have to find a way to effectively interact with one another. This requires governance that takes stock of the broader context. While the IoT does benefit from a certain level of governance such as technical governance in the form of standard it is not at a level that can foster sustained growth as the biggest challenge is to resolve the incompatibility between systems and in some cases accessibility to the data.

The real challenges are to determine how much governance is too much, and to create the right incentives to bring all interested parties to the table. Would this resolve itself due to pressure from consumers and the need for integration and aggregation of data, driving the competition for better solutions?

What Standards Are Needed?

The efficient analysis of big data is enabling better delivery of global healthcare. Health data can help better understand the global burden of disease, efficiently monitor, and evaluate public health efforts. Big data can be quickly analyzed in unprecedented quantities in order to determine patterns and trends. The problem as highlighted earlier is establishing the how and the what, how data is collected and what are the application or use of the data. It is a global problem which has led to officials trying to tackle the problem not only at the national level but also worldwide. For example, the United Nations Global Working Group on big data for Official Statistics is to provide a strategic vision, direction, and coordination for a global programme on big data for official statistics including for indicators of the 2030 Agenda for Sustainable Development. It includes creation of standardized methods for collecting, managing, and processing data securely and ethically, promoting training, and shared experiences.[34] Another good example is the ongoing work from HMA (Heads of Medicines Agency)/EMA (European Medicines Agency) Big Data Steering Group. They are working to enable data-driven decision-making in EMA and across EU, prioritizing ten activities. The aim is to describe the big data landscape from a regulatory perspective and identify practical steps for the European medicines regulatory network to make best use of big data in support of innovation and public health in the European Union (EU).[35] Additionally, the Big Data Steering Group implemented the recommendations of the workplan with its 11 workstreams which will deliver the vision for RWE by 2025. The workplan places emphasis on collaboration across stakeholders and with international regulatory partners. This work also needs to be seen in the wider EU policy context, most notably the European Commission's plans for a European Health Data Space.[36] Talking to Jesper Kjaer from the Danish Health Agency who also co-chairs the Big Data Steering Group explains that the plan is to link and pool different datasets that include raw data pre and post analysis. The source of the raw data will include from the individual or patient level data (un-identifiable), clinical trials, adverse drug reactions, etc. The Steering Group are still evaluating the different standards to use depending on the purpose such as CDISC (Clinical Data Interchange Standards Consortium), FHIR (Fast

Healthcare Interoperability Resources), and OMA (Open Mobile Alliance). These are some of the applications to use big data for market data analysis, safety analysis for scientific advice, and decision-making. This joint taskforce brings new capabilities for EMA and agencies to analyse the data at EU scale and allowing to be available for secondary use (of healthcare data for public health and research purposes). The implementation has started and will be ready in 2025.

Another standard that should be mentioned is ICD (International Statistical Classification of Diseases and Related Health Problems). This is the foundation for the identification of health trends and statistics globally, and the international standard for reporting diseases and health conditions. It is the diagnostic classification standard for all clinical and research purposes. ICD defines the universe of diseases, disorders, injuries, and other related health conditions, listed in a comprehensive, hierarchical fashion that allows for:

- Easy storage, retrieval, and analysis of health information for evidenced-based decision-making.
- Sharing and comparing health information between hospitals, regions, settings, and countries.
- Data comparisons in the same location across different time periods.

Based on clinical input, research, and epidemiology, ICD has become a tool that is suitable for many uses in health for example:

- Monitoring of the incidence and prevalence of diseases
- Causes of death
- Primary care and family medicine concepts.
- Medicines, allergens and chemicals, histopathology.
- Patient safety, in line with the WHO patient safety framework.
- Dual coding for traditional medicine diagnoses.

ICD-11 has been adopted by the Seventy-second World Health Assembly in May 2019 and comes into effect on 1 January 2022.[37]

What Should the Health Data Value Chain Look Like in the Future?

What Is the Patient Data Ecosystem?

Health data is difficult to navigate. As systems and databases are fragmented, aggregating all the data becomes cumbersome. As a result, people might be less engaged and less empowered to improve their health and wellness. The other problem is that organizations need to be transparent on how patient data is or will be used for opt-in (identifiable data) vs. opt-out (anonymized data) type of data. Organizations need to ensure that patients understand and consent to the purpose of the usage of their information. And if changes occur, to allow people to opt out. There needs to be a re-education that patient data is part of a patient's DNA. Also, as a first step to acknowledge that health data generated from health services are paid by and for patients, either directly out of pocket or indirectly through taxes (e.g. national healthcare system). Are patients ready to decide how their data is being used? Do they want to control their data access?

Our concept of the patient data ecosystem is applying the FAIR and TRUST principles by including patients as main stakeholder and to have a seat in the data governance. The importance is finding common benefits and creating a balance of data sharing. In the world where patients own their data, they depend on organizations that are the data controllers or aggregators to control the access, secure their data, maintain information, aggregate various data sources, etc. If these data organizations change their strategy to be more transparent on how they use the patient's data, this might serve as a way of payment to grant them permission for specific purposes as long as the data controllers continue to improve their infrastructure. This could potentially put the trust back into patients and society. It will benefit all data "supporters" in a network as data will be accessible for all stakeholders in the value chain and not only big data organizations like Amazon, IQVIA, Google, etc.

Estrada-Galinanes and Wac classify the systems that manage and preserve health data in a pyramid as seen in Figure 2.3. Individual value is attainable by systems designed for single-user data for example mHealth app. Community value is possible when data is kept in well-curated institutional repositories, for example biobanks. The benefits are subscribed to a group of individuals. Societal value is viable with open, and ideally raw data. Systems that gain space in the upper part of this pyramid can bring social innovation such as rising life expectancy that can significantly impact different fields that need creative solutions to meet social goals.[38]

The value increases from individual to collective to societal. The trust, collaboration, transparency, and data

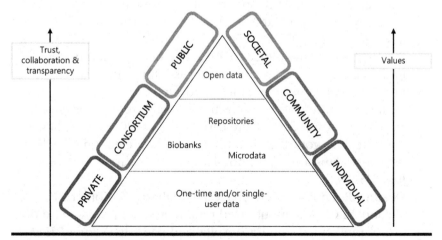

Figure 2.3 Hierarchical value of health data.

protection are requirements in order to reach higher value. There is still a road ahead to overcome all these challenges.

Notes

1 IBM. How to manage complexity and realize the value of big data. IBM Smarter Business Review, https://www.ibm.com/blogs/services/2020/05/28/how-to-manage-complexity-and-realize-the-value-of-big-data/ (accessed June 25, 2021).
2 World Economic Forum. How much data is generated each day? Digital Economy and New Value Creation, https://www.weforum.org/agenda/2019/04/how-much-data-is-generated-each-day-cf4bddf29f/ (accessed June 25, 2021).
3 Garvin E. In-depth: rise of the ePatient movement. HIT Consultant, https://hitconsultant.net/2014/06/25/rise-of-the-epatient-movement/#.YRvX0tOA4-R (accessed August 23, 2021).
4 HealthIT.gov. Medical practice efficiencies & cost savings. Achieve Practice Efficiencies & Cost Savings, https://www.healthit.gov/topic/health-it-and-health-information-exchange-basics/medical-practice-efficiencies-cost-savings (accessed June 25, 2021).
5 BusinessWire. Global Electronic Health Records (EHR) market (2020 to 2025) – by product, component, end-user, region, competition, forecast & opportunities – ResearchAndMarkets.com. Research and Markets, https://www.businesswire.com/news/home/20200527005390/en/Global-Electronic-Health-Records-EHR-Market-2020-to-2025---by-Product-Component-End-user-Region-Competition-Forecast-Opportunities---ResearchAndMarkets.com (accessed June 25, 2021).
6 HealthIT.gov. Adoption of electronic health record systems among US non-federal acute care hospitals: 2008–2015, https://www.healthit.gov/data/data-briefs/adoption-electronic-health-record-systems-among-us-non-federal-acute-care-1 (accessed June 25, 2021).
7 Dexter PR, Perkins S, Overhage JM, Maharry K, Kohler RB, McDonald CJ. A computerized reminder system to increase the use of preventive care for hospitalized patients. *N Engl J Med*. 2001 September 27;345(13):965–970.

8 Kucher N, Koo S, Quiroz R, Cooper JM, Paterno MD, Soukonnikov B, Goldhaber SZ. Electronic alerts to prevent venous thromboembolism among hospitalized patients. *N Engl J Med*. 2005 March 10;352(10):969–977.

9 Bates DW, Leape LL, Cullen DJ, Laird N, Petersen LA, Teich JM, Burdick E, Hickey M, Kleefield S, Shea B, Vander Vliet M, Seger DL. Effect of computerized physician order entry and a team intervention on prevention of serious medication errors. *JAMA*. 1998 October 21;280(15):1311–1316.

10 Amarasingham R, Plantinga L, Diener-West M, Gaskin DJ, Powe NR. Clinical information technologies and inpatient outcomes: a multiple hospital study. *Arch Intern Med*. 2009 January 26;169(2):108–114.

11 Satterfield BA MD PhD, Dikilitas O MD, Kullo IJ MD. Leveraging the electronic health record to address the COVID-19 pandemic. Published: April 21, 2021. doi:10.1016/j.mayocp.2021.04.008 (accessed August 23, 2021).

12 Tapuria A, Porat T, Kalra D, Dsouza G, Xiaohui S, Curcin V. Impact of patient access to their electronic health record: systematic review. *Inform Health Soc Care*. 2021;46(2):194–206. doi:10.1080/17538157.2021.1879810

13 MPR News. Doctors removes cancer patient's one healthy kidney by mistake, https://www.mprnews.org/story/2008/03/18/mistake (accessed August 23, 2021).

14 Mearian L. US doctors don't believe patients need full access to health records. Computerworld, https://www.computerworld.com/article/2496084/u-s--doctors-don-t-believe-patients-need-full-access-to-health-records.html (accessed August 23, 2021).

15 Van Kuppenveld SI, Van Os-medendorp H, Tiemessen NA, Van Delden JJ. Real-time access to electronic health record via a patient portal: is it harmful? A retrospective observational study. *J Med Internet Res*. 2020 February 6;22(2):e13622. PMID: 32044753; PMCID: PMC7055752. doi:10.2196/13622.

16 Lin S, et al. Are patients electronically accessing their medical records? Evidence from national hospital data. *Health Info Technol: Health Aff*. 2009;38:11, https://www.healthaffairs.org/doi/pdf/10.1377/hlthaff.2018.05437 (accessed August 23, 2021).

17 Bechtel C, et al. Why aren't more patients electronically accessing their medical records (yet)? *Health Aff.*, https://www.

healthaffairs.org/do/10.1377/hblog20200108.82072/full/
(accessed August 23, 2021).

18 https://www.beckershospitalreview.com/healthcare-informa-
tion-technology/apple-adds-medical-records-to-its-health-app.
html (accessed June 25, 2021).

19 Lopreite M, Panzarasa P, Puliga M, et al. Early warnings of
COVID-19 outbreaks across Europe from social media. *Sci Rep.*
(2021);11:2147. doi:10.1038/s41598-021-81333-1

20 Apple. Apple advances personal health by introducing secure
sharing and new insights, https://www.apple.com/uk/news-
room/2021/06/apple-advances-personal-health-by-introducing-
secure-sharing-and-new-insights/ (accessed August 25, 2021).

21 Anderson A, et al. Using patient advisory boards to solicit input
into clinical trial design and execution. *Clin Ther.* 2019;42(8),
https://www.clinicaltherapeutics.com/action/showPdf?pi
i=S0149-2918%2819%2930333-9 (accessed November 9, 2021).

22 Ristevski B, Chen M. Big data analytics in medicine and healthcare. *J Integr Bioinform.* 2018;15(3):20170030. doi:10.1515/
jib-2017-0030 (accessed August 23, 2021).

23 HIMSS. Interoperability in healthcare, https://www.himss.org/
resources/interoperability-healthcare (accessed June 25, 2021).

24 Sullivan T. Why EHR data interoperability is such a mess in 3
charts. *Healthcare IT News*, https://www.healthcareitnews.com/
news/why-ehr-data-interoperability-suchmess-3-charts
(accessed June 25, 2021).

25 HIPAA Journal. Healthcare data breach statistics, https://www.
hipaajournal.com/healthcare-data-breach-statistics/ (accessed
November 9, 2021).

26 UK Government. Data protection, https://www.gov.uk/data-
protection (accessed August 23, 2021).

27 Centers for Disease Control and Prevention. Health Insurance
Portability and Accountability Act of 1996 (HIPAA), https://
www.cdc.gov/phlp/publications/topic/hipaa.html (accessed
August 23, 2021).

28 GDPR. Complete guide to GDPR compliance, https://gdpr.eu/
data-privacy/ (accessed August 23, 2021).

29 European Medicines Agency. HMA-EMA joint big data taskforce
phase II report: 'evolving data-driven regulation', https://www.
ema.europa.eu/en/documents/other/hma-ema-joint-big-data-
taskforce-phase-ii-report-evolving-data-driven-regulation_en.pdf
(accessed August 23, 2021).

30 Luciano F, Mariarosaria T. What is data ethics? *Phil Trans R Soc.* 2016;A.3742016036020160360, http://doi.org/10.1098/rsta.2016.0360 (accessed August 23, 2021).

31 Open Knowledge Foundation. What is open data. Open Data Handbook, http://opendatahandbook.org/guide/en/what-is-open-data/ (accessed June 24, 2021).

32 Lin D, Crabtree J, Dillo I, et al. The TRUST principles for digital repositories. *Sci Data.* 2020;7:144. doi:10.1038/s41597-020-0486-7 (accessed June 28, 2021).

33 Boeckhout M, Zielhuis GA, Bredenoord AL. The FAIR guiding principles for data stewardship: fair enough? *Eur J Hum Genet.* 2018;26(7):931–936. doi:10.1038/s41431-018-0160-0 (accessed June 28, 2021).

34 United Nations. Mandate and terms of reference of the UN-CEBD. UN Committee of Experts on big data and Data Science for Official Statistics, https://unstats.un.org/bigdata/about/mandate.cshtml (accessed August 22, 2021).

35 European Medicines Agency. Big data. HMA/EMA Big Data Steering Group, https://www.ema.europa.eu/en/about-us/how-we-work/big-data#hma/ema-big-data-steering-group-section (accessed August 22, 2021).

36 Arlett P, et al. Real-world evidence in EU medicines regulation: enabling use and establishing value. *Am Soc Clin Pharmacol Ther.*, https://ascpt.onlinelibrary.wiley.com/doi/10.1002/cpt.2479 (accessed November 24, 2021).

37 World Health Organization. International statistical classification of diseases and related health problems (ICD), https://www.who.int/standards/classifications/classification-of-diseases (accessed August 23, 2021).

38 Estrada-Galinanes V, Wac K. Visions and challenges in managing and preserving data to measure quality of life. 2018 IEEE 3rd International Workshops on Foundations and Applications of Self* Systems (FAS*W), 2018, pp. 92–99. doi:10.1109/FAS-W.2018.00031 (accessed June 30, 2021).

Chapter 3

The Value of Health Data for Patients

How Do Patients See Their Health Data?

In healthcare, there has always been a tension between the
need to share health data and the need to protect it because
of its sensitive nature. In the next section of this book, we will
explore the public perception on this delicate balance to
understand what citizens expect when it comes to their
personal health data.

Patients Are Overall Open to Sharing Their Data…

In 2019, the European Union conducted a Eurobarometer[1]
titled: Attitudes towards the impact of digitalization on daily
lives. In this report, an entire section was dedicated to citizen's
perception and preferences with regard to sharing their
personal data. The 60% of respondents said they would be
willing to share their personal information if it helped the
public service. Among them, 43% specifically said they would
share their data if it were to improve medical research and

DOI:10.4324/9781003215868-3

care. However, it is noteworthy that more than one-third of respondents affirmed that they were not willing to share any personal information for any purposes.

But what influences such decisions? The Eurobarometer included a socio-demographic analysis of the respondents that showed that the younger the respondents, the higher placed on the social ladder, and the more educated, the more willing they are to share their personal information. Those with financial problems and precarious jobs are, in contrast, less likely to share their data.

It is quite clear that the public willingness to share their personal information highly depends on the purpose for which it will be used. According to the Eurobarometer, improving medical research and care are goals that citizens are willing to contribute by sharing their data. In our discussion with patients, it clearly appeared that there is a consensus around the idea of sharing health data for medical research. These results are confirmed by other systematic reviews that all suggest that willingness to share data is high when it comes to supporting research, as benefits are well understood by citizens.[2] Furthermore, studies in the US suggest that patients are ready to share their data for as many research studies as possible,[3] an observation that is also present in Canada where patients recognized the benefits of routinely collected medical data for research.[4] In the UK, public acceptance of data sharing went even further as study participants felt positive about sharing anonymized data with health authorities for treatment evaluations[5] and public research.[6]

The main motivation behind the willingness to share data for medical research and care is the feeling of contributing to the common good.[7] For patients in particular, data altruism is essential to improve health outcomes and care for their peers and for generations to come, just as they have themselves benefited from the patients that came before them. Indeed, advancements in medicine lie on the data collected, shared, and processed by generations of patients, health professionals, and scientists before us. Today, patients feel a sense of responsibility to continue to do so and support research. Furthermore, patients understand quite well the benefits of data sharing, as highlighted by their responses in various studies: improve medical decision-making, improve diagnosis and treatment plans, find new treatments, and empower innovation.

...although They Understand the Risks

While they understand the benefits of sharing their data for research, patients also have a sense of the risks that come with data sharing. Across the world, patients reported fear of data thefts by hackers, or data falling into the wrong hands and being misused by commercial organizations for financial gains. A pan-European study confirmed this observation by showing that patients felt comfortable with medical professionals accessing their health data but were strongly averse to insurance or pharmaceutical companies viewing that same information.[8] Even within the medical team, patients don't feel the same level of comfort sharing their health data depending on the recipient. Indeed, a study showed that the level of comfort patients felt with regard to sharing their data was correlated to the level of professional training a member of the medical team had. As an example, participants in the study were more open to sharing their data with pharmacists than with pharmacy assistants. Talking to patients, we received confirmation that nearly all of them feel comfortable sharing their health data with their GP or their hospital. However, as soon as they are asked if they would share their information outside the medical setting, they become very reluctant. We therefore tried to understand why, by asking them if they knew how their health data is used. To our surprise most of them had no idea. In fact, we realized that there is a lot of misunderstanding over how health data is used outside of the medical environment. This lack of understanding is often filled with speculation, fear, and reluctance.

During interviews, data brokers told us that a key difference that needs to be understood is that between identifiable data and anonymized data. When patients fear their data might be stolen or misused, they usually talk about their identifiable data. Indeed, this is the type of data that exposes them personally to commercial targeting by companies or blackmail by hackers. Therefore, it is coherent to want more data protection for identifiable information. But should the same apply to anonymized data?

Often, patients fear that their sensitive health data might be accessed by unauthorized third parties, putting them at risk. In October 2020, the medical records of thousands of patients attending a psychotherapy facility were stolen and used to blackmail them.[9] Those records contained information about therapy sessions, care plans as well as social security numbers and addresses. Some of the patients even received emails threatening them to publicly reveal the content of their medical records if they didn't pay the blackmailer.

Such incidents leave patients fearing for their own integrity because their personal identifiable data is at risk of being exposed. However, health data experts warn that patients should be informed that in health research, most information is anonymized. This means that any identifiable information such as the name, the date of birth, or the address is usually removed. Data privacy has always been a major preoccupation in medical ethics. Biomedical research has therefore always been submitted to strict rules to preserve patient's privacy and make sure that anonymization techniques make re-identification difficult. In addition, the methodologies that guide research compels organizations to obtain results that are representative of a target population, not of a specific individual. Therefore, identifiable data is usually of little use when it comes to scientific research. In the cases in which identifiable data is needed, depending on the country and the local regulation, explicit and written consent from the patient is sought. Hence, in most cases, researchers, whether they come from public organizations or private ones (pharmaceutical companies, CROs, etc.) are mostly interested in analyzing the behaviour and characteristics of populations and not of particular individuals. For instance, a pharmaceutical company might want to understand what are the adverse reactions that individuals using their product experience. To do so, they will pull together large volumes of anonymized data representative of that population and analyse the results. Knowing who each individual in that cohort is doesn't add any value.

The confusion between the use of identifiable and anonymized data is legitimate and stems from a misunderstanding of the way biomedical research works. In addition, this confusion is maintained by the fact that, according to a 2019 Public Opinion Strategies study, 46% of Americans noticed online advertising for a health condition they have, creating suspicion regarding the way their health data is handled by commercial companies. But it is important to note that the fields of advertising and medical research are based on very different approaches. Advertising works on precise consumer targeting, whereas medical research works on a populational basis.

Health data experts highlighted during our discussions that it is important for patients to understand the difference between their identifiable and their anonymized data because this distinction can lead to drastically different data use frameworks. Indeed, when it comes to identifiable data, patients should be given strong access restriction rights to preserve their privacy and their integrity. This is partially addressed by various international regulations such as the

GDPR. However, when it comes to anonymized data, many health data experts feel like the access conditions should be much more flexible. Indeed, since patients aren't exposed to the risk of being identified, data should circulate with much for fluidity to facilitate research.

Hence, educating patients about the way the health data ecosystem works could reassure them with regard to the way their health data is used.

These two key elements show that data sharing isn't so much about the nature and content of the information at stake, as it is about the purpose for which it is shared and the entity using it. There is however one exception: mental health data. Participants in a study mentioned that they were only comfortable sharing their health data when they were in an unstable mental condition because it could help them, and others keep safe. In a stable state, they would want less information sharing because no one's safety is at risk. Similarly, another participant expressed concerns about the risk for stigma and discrimination of mental health data such as prescriptions were made available beyond the medical team (to employers, for instance).

Principles of Safe Data Sharing

There is an extensive body of literature about the patient perspective on health data and their preferences when it comes to data sharing. Ultimately, it all comes down to the level of trust they place in an organization or an individual (Figure 3.1).

This trust depends on various factors:

- Transparency: the main worry patients have when sharing their data is understanding how it is going to be used and by whom. Therefore, being transparent on the collection, storage, and processing of health

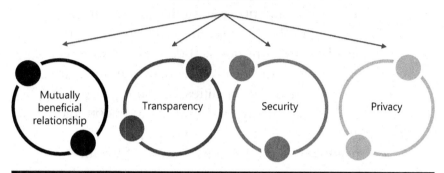

Figure 3.1 Trust factors.

data is key in creating a trust relationship that encourages data sharing. Transparency also involves informing patients about their rights such as the possibility to withdraw access to their personal information. A study shows that 45% of respondents said they were more likely to participate in a clinical trial if they were given clear information about the use of their data.[10] Despite transparency being a key concern for patients, the 2019 Public Opinion Strategies report shows that 30% of Americans believe their health data has been shared without their knowledge. Interestingly, 66% of respondents believe that their data might have been shared without them knowing by and with their insurance company. In addition, almost half of them also believe that health data related to their online activities is shared with technology companies without them knowing. This data points out that although patients cannot directly identify the inner workings of the health data industry, they sense that some stakeholders hold back information and lack transparency on their practices.

■ Security: it goes without saying that personal health information should always be stored in a secure way that prevents unauthorized third parties from accessing it. But how secure is secure enough? Considering recent hospital data breaches, it is legitimate to wonder if current security measures, especially in health facilities, are strict enough and create a trustworthy environment to encourage patient data sharing.

■ Privacy: given the sensitive nature of health information, privacy should be the number 1 priority of any organization collecting, processing, sharing, or storing data. As described by Gartner in a 2020 report, privacy will become a key customer concern, just as "cruelty-free" or "organic" have been before.[11] But more than just a trend, privacy will become one of the biggest battle horses of regulators worldwide. According to this same report, in 2023, 65% of the world's population will have its personal information covered by a privacy regulation, from 10% in 2020.

■ A mutually beneficial relationship: most patients believe that both themselves and the organizations they share their data with should benefit from this agreement. Some argue that if they agree to share their data for research, they should be given access to the results and presented the implication of these results for them and their peers. They place their trust in the system that will make sure that positive outcomes emerge from the use of their data. Others expect financial compensation. This last point will be further discussed in this book.

Talking to patients and patient representatives, we realized that although all of them agreed on these principles, they had different visions on how data sharing should be implemented in practice. Some considered that patients should fully own their data, meaning they should have entire control over their personal health information. Others considered that data is a public good, belonging collectively, and should therefore be freely available with simple patient consent. On this spectrum, each person we talked to had a slightly different position, illustrating the complexity behind a very simple question: Whose data is it anyway?

Whose Data Is It Anyway?

Despite the important role data privacy took in the public debate, only 46% of Eurobarometer respondents stated that they wish to take a more active role in controlling their data while 38% said the opposite. This opens the debate about a quite controversial topic: Who should own (and control) health data? The question of data ownership is tightly linked to the emergence of digital data and its value. Back when all health data was written on paper and kept by physicians in their offices, patients were confident that it wasn't used or shared much. With digital data, accessibility is much higher for organizations across the world, under different forms and for different purposes, generating revenue. This is when data ownership became a problem. As patients became aware of the benefits of sharing "their data", they also became aware of its risks. Moreover, the financial value generated by health data also left some patients wondering why they weren't benefiting from it, as rightful data subjects. Concerns over data privacy coupled with a feeling of unjustly being taken advantage of financially lead some patients wanting more control over their data. In other words, patients started claiming data ownership.

During our interviews, we asked many stakeholders who owns health data in their opinion. Many answered in a very confident way "Patients own their data!". To them, data "about me" was a synonym of "my data". But what exactly does it mean to own something, and can patients actually own their health data? The answer is not that simple.

The definition of ownership can vary depending on the jurisdiction but, generally, it refers to the right to possess something. From a legal perspective, the situation is quite complex depending on the country or even within the country. For instance, in some American states, it is stated that patients own all their health data including their medical records, while in other states patients own their health data but as soon as part of it is included in medical records kept by healthcare providers, it becomes their property.[12] On the opposite, in countries such as France, no one can claim ownership over medical records as it is not an asset that can be possessed by anyone.

In today's healthcare industry, many different stakeholders claim "ownership" over health data, outside of patients. It can be physicians who collect the information in the context of care and place it in electronic health records. It can be researchers who put together and maintain databases for their studies. It can also be data companies that purchase or collect information to transform it into insights for private companies or governments, who in turn use these insights to guide policies and corporate strategies. It could even be social media platforms or traditional media that are both a source of health data and a way to broadcast research results. In other words, in healthcare, the amount of people and organizations involved in the data value chain is significant. Their roles and responsibilities are intricate and inter-dependent, making it sometimes hard to assign specific roles to each of them. Many of them even claim ownership over the data because they consider they have furnished efforts and made financial investments to collect, process, or store the information. Figure 3.2 describes the different roles that should be considered when managing, accessing, or processing the data.

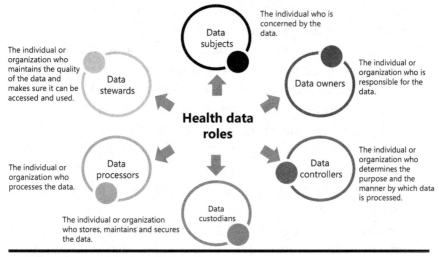

Figure 3.2   Health data roles.

In addition, data is rarely just about an individual. Although it relates to a patient's health it also contains information about the medical team and the health facility. It holds data used by insurances to pay for care, it holds information used by pharmaceutical companies to develop drugs. Almost all stakeholders have an interest in owning a slice of the health data cake. In some jurisdictions roles are clearly defined and some other leave room for interpretation. Either way, the fight for health data ownership is still ongoing and nothing points with certainty to a patient victory.

Own Your Data to Keep It Private

Let's imagine we are in an environment in which patients can legally own their health data. What does it entail? First of all, owning something provides an individual with rights and responsibilities. When it comes to health data, patients would be given the right to restrict access to their data, decide with whom they want to share it and for what use and even request to be compensated for lending their personal information. Ideally, patients could have full visibility over every entity who requires access to their data, whether identifiable or anonymized, and grant or refuse access. That would allow them to choose the subjects they wish to contribute to and the stakeholders they wish to collaborate with. This could come in the form of a web portal which lists all the different databases that hold a patient's data and enable them to control access to said information. That would create locks that only the patient would be able to remove if they wish to.

However, in practice, it is nearly impossible to expect patients to have full control over their data. That would imply that they must be clearly informed each time their data, whether identifiable or not, is used. Once they are informed, they then need to provide consent and "unlock" access to data. Such a system would not only be impossible for patients to manage but it would also collapse the entire healthcare industry. Doctors wouldn't be able to access and share critical information for their patient's care when needed, researchers would struggle to conduct their studies, drastically slowing down medical advancements, pharmaceutical companies would increase development times due to a lack of data and governments would struggle to pilot effective strategies. Patients, on the other hand, would spend all their time reading consent forms and granting permissions. People rarely exercise the control they already have on their personal information. For instance, they almost never read the terms and conditions before making a purchase, or simply click on "agree all" instead of reading the cookie policy on websites. Of course, this behaviour is often due to lengthy forms that are hard to understand, but would patients really take the time to fully manage their health data? Some might not want to, others might consider that the task is too complex, and they lack the skills to fully understand the implications of their actions.

Through interviews and research, we concluded that it is practically impossible to expect patients to be the sole owners of their health data. Although the rights that come with health data ownership seem seductive, the responsibilities place an overwhelming and unethical burden on patients. Instead, health data can be co-owned by different stakeholders. Take the example of lab results: patients are the source of data. But this data can only be generated when a health professional draws blood and sends it to a lab. There, another professional turns blood into numbers, generating the first interpretable set of data. But that is not all. A physician will apply its knowledge and experience to these numbers to generate insights and provide their patient with a diagnosis. That diagnosis will be recorded in a database and sent to insurance companies that will reimburse the patient, the hospital, or the lab. As it turns out, that patient had diabetes, so their data will also be used in populational studies to determine new diabetes risk factors. The list of ways health data travels between multiple stakeholders and is used is infinite. Some collect data, others aggregate it, others store it, others process it, others even add themselves to the party in order to regulate all these data flows. Data cannot be owned by a single party. Rather, health data calls for a shared ownership governance model, involving each stakeholder.

The Shared Ownership Governance Model

The shared ownership governance model has two levels of application: in data management organizations and in the general public. When it comes to data management organizations, patient representatives advocate for a more inclusive decision-making process. Indeed, patients should not only be considered as data subjects, but they should also be given a sit at the table to advocate for their rights and represent the public's interest. For instance, patients could be included in data project validation boards or in strategic working groups. When it comes to the general public, the expectations are clear: patients want to be informed on the way their health data is used. Although most of them do not wish to have full control over their data, they do want to be given clear and understandable information on the way their personal data is collected, processed, and further shared. In addition, patients increasingly expect to be informed of the outcomes produced by the studies their data was used for.

In a nutshell, the shared ownership governance model provides patients with a share of voice whether within official organizations or as simple citizens in the management of their health data. It is safe to say that the more patients will have access to educational resources about their health data, the more active they will want to be in managing their sensitive information. Just like with their care, the more empowered patients are, the more meaningfully they will be able to contribute to the system. This shift needs to be anticipated. While some of the experts we talked to confirmed that only a minority of educated patients are preoccupied by their health data, we believe that the situation will soon evolve. As the topic of data protection, ownership or monetization will take centre stage in the public debate, patients will want to know more about the way their health data is handled. Health organizations will not be able to keep on hiding behind lengthy and unreadable consent forms, opaque practices, and undisclosed deals. Transparency will need to become the norm.

The Social Licence to Use Data

In order to be accepted and trusted by patients, health data applications need not only to comply with the latest data protection and patient information regulations, but they also need to obtain a social licence.[13] The idea of a social licence for the use of health data was developed to illustrate the fact that citizen's expectations can go far beyond what is legally asked of health data users. If citizens do not consider that a data user is trustworthy, acts in the public's best interest or shares values of reciprocity, they might refuse to share their health data even though all other legal requirements were fulfilled. The power of the public perception and of the social licence must not be underestimated. Even in systems where trust in public organizations or in medical communities is high, taking the public's acceptance for granted can be a fatal mistake. This is what happened in the UK, when NHS England decided to launch care.data, a large database of primary and secondary care data for research. First, reports and news articles indicate that most citizens were not informed that this programme was being developed, which is considered very odd for an initiative of this magnitude.[14] Moreover, the NHS took the controversial decision to share the data collected with private companies after it had asked the public if they wanted to opt out. In other words, citizens were asked to decide on whether or not they wanted to share their health data before even knowing who it was going to be shared with. Finally, the NHS admitted that it had not made sufficient effort to explain the benefits of this database and the ways health data could support research. Despite being in full compliance with the regulation and usually earning the public's trust, the NHS failed to receive the social licence to develop care.data. This can be explained by two factors: the operation lacked transparency and the public perceived the NHS's interests to be divergent from their own.

Trusted Environments

Instead of placing the burden on patients to assume the control of their health data, why not place the burden on the system to create regulations, frameworks, and guidelines strong enough that patients accept to share their data without fear? That would amount to creating trusted environments designed with a high level of data protection, patient information, and social licence. These trusted environments can be, for instance, national data-sharing platforms dedicated to biomedical research or cohort studies developed by patient organizations. Overall, these are environments patients trust because they act in the public's best interest and follow strict data protection guidelines. Instead of having to look after their data themselves, patients could place their trust in these environments and rest assured that their data is properly taken care of.

The reasoning can be taken even further and consider that in such environments, data sharing is automatic, based on an opt-out system, rather than an opt-in as it is usually the case today. Indeed, in many countries, depending on the envisioned use, patients need to provide their consent before sharing their data with a third party. Although this is perfectly understandable, it does create obstacles when it comes to research. Indeed, such opt-in scenarios create burdens for researchers and lengthen the duration of their studies. When considering that patients generally agree to share their health data for public research, initiatives within this scope could have automatic access to data.

In Europe, the GDPR created an exemption that allows each country to determine if patients still need to provide their consent for the secondary use of their data in the context of research. According to a study conducted in Germany, patients are massively willing to give wide consent for the secondary research use of their health data (93%) and 75% of them even agree to fully suppress consent in this context.[15] However, talking to Gözde Susuzlu, project manager at Data Saves Lives, we realized that not all European citizens place the same amount of trust in their public institutions, and some are not data savvy enough to feel comfortable giving up control over their health data.

Nevertheless, the GDPR paved the ground for more flexible data frameworks when it comes to research. Coupled with the other data protection and patient information requirements, this could lead to the creation of trusted environments that would allow researchers to work within a standardized and less constraining framework. In return, patients can be given visibility over the studies that are performed using their health data, and if necessary, they can opt-out of the system. These trusted frameworks are a way of addressing the health data dilemma: they both protect patient privacy and provide researchers with a facilitated access to data.

Patients Are Not Cash Cows

Patients may consider unfair the way value derived from health data processing is shared. Indeed, most of the time they provide their health data for free while other organizations down the line generate important revenues with it. Steven Petrow was 26 years old when he was diagnosed with testicular cancer. During his treatment, the hospital collected a sample of his tumour and other bodily parts. Years later, he read that the same hospital decided to grant access to medical records and biological samples to private companies in exchange for a significant sum of money. Steven, as many other patients in the same situation, found this deeply upsetting.

Many companies argue that raw data is of no value. What creates the value of health data is the way it is collected, cleaned, stored, or processed. For instance, the cost of implementing an EHR system in a healthcare facility can exceed $1 billion, considering the initial setup and the yearly maintenance fees. Data brokerage companies also heavily invest in servers to store data, in software to process it and in people to generate insights. Patients, on the other hand, do nothing. No investments, no efforts. They simply need to be to generate health data. As a consequence, many stakeholders consider that patients should not be compensated for their data because they create no value. Some do say, however, that they would be ready to pay patients if they were to take the time to fill out surveys or contribute to cleaning their data or qualify it. In other words, those who generate value can receive value.

However, this logic has its limits, and it suffices to transpose it to other assets to understand it. Imagine you inherit a piece of land. You have done nothing to own it, other than being born in the right family. No investments, no effort. As it turns out, your soil is not only incredibly fertile, but it also holds precious stones and is ideally located to build a successful hotel business. The "health data logic" would want you to freely give away your land to farmers, gemologists, and hotel companies to conduct their business. But, once someone holds something of value, they are entitled to receive compensation when that thing is made available to others. So, in the real world, you would rent part of your land to farmers, you would ask for a commission on the gems extracted, and you would probably sell the remaining part to a hotel business. You created no particular value, yet you still benefited financially from the value your land generated.

Another great example is oil. The analogy is particularly relevant as on many occasions data has been named "the new oil" in reference to its incalculable value. But oil, like many other raw materials, has an intrinsic value before ever being processed. It cannot be used in its initial state, just like raw data, but that doesn't mean it is worthless.

It can also be argued that individual data is of no use and that value is only created when combined with other data. For instance, knowing that a patient experienced an adverse reaction to a treatment is much more valuable when merged with data from other patients to understand if this is just an isolated event or if it is a frequent complication of a treatment.

No matter how you see things, theory needs to be put into practice. Often, this is where difficulties emerge. For one, as discussed above, some countries simply forbid patients to be compensated for their data. In those who authorize it, the question is: How do we define the value of health data for patients and the economic model associated with it?

So, let's envision a world where patients would be compensated for their health data. Just like with data ownership, there is no easy way to put theory into practice and although compensating patients for their health data seems like a good idea, it might be nothing more than a utopia. Indeed, allowing patients to monetize their data would necessitate the creation of a complex system to assess the fair value of each information and redistribute the money generated. Moreover, in order to do so, each data set would need to be linked to a patient's identity in order to allow the financial transactions to take place. That would create further privacy threats that are reduced when data is anonymized and therefore decorrelated from a patient's identity.

But the complexity didn't discourage certain companies from creating data monetization models for patients. These are called data marketplaces. Patients create their online medical record into which they can pour all their existing information. If a data user such as a research organization or a pharmaceutical company wants access to this information, they can send the patient a purchase offer. These models only work if the platform has sufficient users for clients to collect large volumes of data. As argued above, individual information has very little value in research.

The Social Vision

During our interviews, two drastically different visions came in conflict. Those who saw their health data as a tradable good and those who saw it as a public good. For the first group of people, health data is just a regular commodity that can be exchanged, purchased, or sold. They defended the vision presented at the beginning of this section. The other group, however, defended a more collective vision of health data.

By definition, health data can be considered as a non-rivalrous transactional good, meaning that it can be used by many entities at the same time without affecting its supply. Indeed, data can easily be duplicated and used by many different stakeholders across the globe while still being available for us when needed. Because it is so largely consumed and impacts so many aspects of healthcare, it is difficult to have an individualistic approach to health data. In public health systems, many patients consider that since they don't pay for their care, they shouldn't expect the system to compensate them for sharing their data. It is a public good that fuels a public system based on solidarity.

In reality, only a small percentage of patients wish to be financially compensated for their health data. A European study showed that only 9% to 17% of participants would share their health data in exchange for a financial incentive. Perhaps these figures are greater on the other side of the Atlantic, but they show that the reasons citizens usually agree to share their health data has nothing to do with money. As we heard during interviews, helping others, and contributing to the greater good had no price.

Tech to the Rescue

Blockchain, a Tool for a Shared Ownership Governance Model

A blockchain is a distributed ledger shared among multiple stakeholders, with two main characteristics: decentralization and immutability. Decentralization distinguishes blockchain from other technologies used to store and manage information, such that before blockchain, data management used to be centralized, with data inserted in databases controlled by central administrators (belonging to specific companies). In the traditional centralized data management scenario, one cannot strictly guarantee the integrity of that data management, hence the integrity of the stored information which is shared among stakeholders that may have divergent interests and different reasons to seek that integrity. The value proposition of a blockchain decentralized system is to create mathematical trust in the data that sits on the ledger and ensure no manipulation is possible. Because the ledger is distributed among various stakeholders, every new information that is added is transparent, incentivizing each organization to play by the rules as seen in Figure 3.3.

Blockchains are purpose-built to solve issues of trust, transparency, and incentive alignment. It creates a unique source of truth so that all parties within the network stay in sync. Blockchains are particularly useful in a context of lack

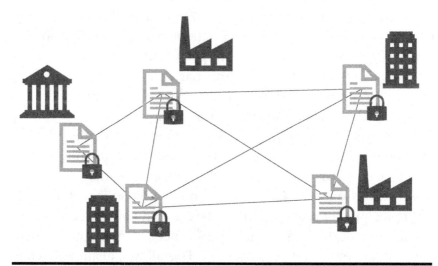

Figure 3.3 The distributed ledger.

of trust and difficult data reconciliation but also when there is a real case – such as economic – for disintermediation.

By providing a tamper-proof ledger of identity, content, and chronology, the technology can have a great impact on business processes and smooth exchanges at the scale of large networks of organizations.

Blockchain can be a private platform with vetted participants or a public open network, such as Bitcoin, where anyone can participate in the maintenance of the ledger.

But not all data or information can be stored in blockchain. It requires off-chain technologies to enable it to access data sources. It needs a risk assessment of what data will be on-the-chain vs. off-the-chain. This would offer more protection compared to other available solutions.

As an immutable digital ledger, the blockchain is an excellent tool for restoring trust between several actors with divergent interests. In the health sector in particular, there is a glaring lack of trust between patients and other actors, especially when it comes to the use of health data. What could the blockchain bring, then?

First, the blockchain can serve as a tamper-proof and time-stamped audit trail to trace a set of transactions. This could be, for example, consent given by a patient, the anonymization of a data set, or its transfer to a third party. The entire data lifecycle can thus be followed transparently by patients. Since no one can intervene to modify this register, the patient can have complete confidence in the traceability data.

At the same time, the blockchain can also allow the implementation of smart contracts to define access rules to health data. Smart contracts are short programs that automatically execute an action when a condition is met. For example, a patient may decide to object to certain treatments or certain uses of their data. These preferences, written into a smart contract, are executed automatically. This allows, again, to create a framework of confidence as to the future of health data.

Thus, the blockchain would create a framework of trust between all health players. With more visibility on the use made of their health data and the possibility of objecting to certain treatments, patients become more sovereign over their personal information. In addition, transparency can become a strong argument to encourage patients to continue to share their health data in a secure environment and thus fight against mistrust. Although blockchain is not a solution on its own, it remains a powerful tool to create "trust by design" in the healthcare sector. Coupled with an educational approach and a real process of transparency vis-à-vis the general public, it is able to help restore a degree of trust between patients and stakeholders in the health sector.

Health Data as NFTs

NFTs are digital non-fungible tokens. Fungible means that one asset can be substituted for another while maintaining the same value. A euro coin and another euro coin are fungible. They can be exchanged between them while keeping the same value. In contrast, non-fungible assets cannot be traded with each other. They are unique and have a specific value that is different from other similar assets. This is the case of artwork. Each piece is unique and has a different intrinsic value to another similar work, or even a copy. While both examples refer to physical assets that are tangible, fungible, and non-fungible assets also exist in the digital world. It could be, for example, an album of the group Kings of Leon, a work of the artist Beeple, or even virtual characters like the CryptoKitties. Take the example of a cryptoart piece like CryptoPunks. This asset is represented by a non-fungible token, similar to a certificate of authenticity registered on a blockchain. Linking this piece to a token, itself linked to a blockchain, makes it possible to keep an unfalsifiable trace of its origin and to trace it over time, in order, for example, to certify its authenticity.

The idea of non-fungible tokens or NFTs is quite revolutionary. Until now, to transfer information between two Internet users, it was only possible to transfer copies of this information. From text to videos, to audio files, everything can be easily duplicated and sent to another person. The recipient, as well as the sender, is most often left with a copy of the digital asset. Until now, there was no mechanism to transfer value online without duplicating content. This posed no particular problem if it was emails or a simple vacation photo between two relatives. But from the moment it was necessary to transfer unique assets or create scarcity, the Internet showed its limits.

So, this is where blockchain and NFTs come in. Each digital asset can be linked to a digital token that lives on the blockchain and cannot be duplicated. Thus, when it comes to transferring an NFT and the asset associated with it, it is the ownership of that asset that is transferred and not a simple digital copy. In other words, blockchain and NFTs are creating scarcity in the digital world.

As discussed above, blockchain technology has the ability to guarantee the integrity of health data. With the arrival of NFTs, blockchain is acquiring an additional tool to meet patients' needs. Indeed, in the future, each medical information could be represented by an NFT. This NFT would be proof that an individual or organization owns the underlying data. Instead of sharing copies and losing track of their data once it has been shared, patients could freely decide to transfer ownership of their data to a third party, such as a medical institution, healthcare professional, or to any person they trust.

Therefore, NFTs could be used as proof of the origin of data and allow the patient to finally have more control over their medical data. In countries that allow it, NFTs could even represent proof of ownership, much like a deed for real estate. It is therefore easy to imagine that this data could then even be sold, thus allowing patients to benefit from a financial gain linked to the use of their health data.

However, it is important to clarify that considering health data as NFTs does not mean that each data will be unique and that it will be impossible to make copies. It simply means that the individual originating the data will be identified and will have increased control over their information. They can then authorize the copy, transfer, and use as needed.

Privacy-Preserving Technologies

Addressing the need for more trust and transparency over the use of data through access control technologies is addressing only one aspect of the problem. The other one is keeping data secure and preserving a patient's privacy. This is where secure computing technologies come into play. Most of them are based on cryptography and ensure that an individual's privacy is preserved all while allowing researchers around the world to analyse their data. Indeed, these technologies make it possible for users to process and analyse data without ever seeing it and provide a technological solution to the health data dilemma: protecting privacy while facilitating access. They are called "homomorphic encryption" or "trusted execution" environments and they all provide the means to securely play with data without compromising a patient's privacy. When using these techniques, only the aggregated results are made available to researchers, and never the raw information itself.

But privacy-preserving technologies can take us step even further by reducing the need to share data with researchers altogether. Today, data is duplicated time and time again in multiple databases depending on the needs. When data is duplicated, errors can occur, and quality can be deteriorated. The more data changes hands, the more risks there are to alter it. So, instead of duplicating and sending data to third parties, why couldn't we allow these third parties to send their processing tools where the data is. These tools are called federated technologies. They allow researchers to analyze data (federated analytics) or train their machine learning models (federated learning) across many devices and databases without having to duplicate and centralize data. For instance, researchers can apply data science methods on datasets that are locally stored in a hospital or a patient's device without requesting a copy of the dataset.

One of the first mainstream examples of federated learning is the next word prediction system that some keyboards now have. To create these systems, engineers have created a basic prediction model that has then been sent to devices in order to learn each individual's way of writing and making personalized predictions. The alternative would have been to simply centralize all personal messages into the provider's cloud system and train their model on that dataset. But in order to preserve users' privacy and make personalized next word suggestions, providers decided to use a federated learning technique. Not only does it improve the model itself, but it also reassures users that their data remains stored locally on their phones. As we are writing this book, researchers are actively working on similar applications in the medical world.

Advancing with Purpose

Writing this chapter, we understood that, at the end of the day, data sharing is not so much about ownership and monetization as it is about purpose. When it comes to our health, many of us act based on what we consider to be "the right way" of doing things. We agree to share our health data for research because we know we contribute to the greater good. On the contrary, we refuse to share our data for commercial purposes because we feel like this model only benefits a few, to the detriment of many. So, what if instead of focusing on controlling data, we focused on defining, as a society, what is acceptable and what is not. In other words, what if we focused on the purpose for which we want our health data to be made available. Once we settle on this and we put in place a shared ownership governance model, we can sleep well knowing that trustworthy third parties defend the common interests we have set. Sounds like a utopia? Here are some initial thinking points to move into this direction:

- Build trusted environments around consensual use cases.
- Generate leadership through an inclusive and representative organization that will define the new "right way" of doing things. Just as we are able to reach consensus of the most appropriate strategies to treat a disease, chances are we will be able to reach consensus on the way different health data use cases need to be addressed.
- Create educational resources to help citizens understand the new stakes and take part in the public debate.
- Communicate the reasons why health data is so important instead of addressing privacy and security concerns.
- Be transparent every step of the way to build public trust.

MINI CASE STUDY 3.1: RETURNING RESULTS TO PATIENTS

In the patient interviews we have conducted ourselves while writing this book, we realized that helping others is a key motivator when it comes to data sharing. However, that doesn't mean that patients don't expect anything in return, as illustrated by this discussion we had with Guillemette Jacob, Founder of Seintinelles, a French association that empowers patients to contribute to medical research by sharing their data.

Seintinelles is a community of patients that volunteer to complete online surveys for different health and medical studies. Once a user signs up to the platform they receive an email each time a researcher is looking for participants in a study. If the user meets the inclusion criteria, they are asked to fill out a survey that will provide researchers with qualitative data for their study. This platform easily connects researchers with patients and helps tackle one of the most important challenges in medical research: finding participants.

> What we try to achieve, although we are only just starting, is a co-construction model between researchers and patients. We realized that researchers have a lot of dead angles that patients can help with if they are involved in the project early on. Take the example of surveys about the quality of life in patients suffering from cancer. If you ask researchers to list the items that they believe are important to evaluate the quality of life, you will see that they can drastically differ from the items patients list. In general, researchers only find 80% of the items that patients list. This means that 20% of the items are in their dead angle but patients are here to compensate for that.

During our discussion, we asked Guillemette Jacob if the patients who participate in these surveys often ask questions about the way their health data is processed. Her answer was quite surprising:

> No. No one ever asked me what happens to the data once it is collected through the survey.

> In fact, what patients care about is the end ben-
> efit, the result. What happens in between is a
> black box, they feel like it is too complicated,
> and they don't really want to know. We only give
> them a couple of guarantees that we will protect
> the privacy and security of their health data, but
> they don't ask for more.

Talking to Guillemette Jacob, we understood that the reason Seintinelles patients don't ask questions about the way their data is processed is because they trust the organization. The platform is very transparent on the two most important conditions patients have when sharing their data: who uses the data and for what purpose? Patients are given comprehensive information about the research organization behind each study and are explained the reasons why each survey is conducted. The effort accomplished to create transparency on these aspects reassures patients. They feel like their data lies in a safe environment even if they don't fully understand the machinery behind it. Guillemette also pointed out that one of the reasons patients trust her platform is because they only work with public research organizations. She knows that, unfortunately, if she brings private entities into the platform, like pharmaceutical companies, she is at risk of breaking the trust relationship she built with her community. The middle ground she found is to only work with pharmaceutical companies if they are associated with public organizations. When that happens, she informs participants that a private company is involved in the study to allow them to make an informed decision.

In addition to knowing who uses their data and for what purpose, Seintinelles patients want to be given access to the results of the study. The problem is that sometimes, researchers are more interested in what the result is rather than what they can do with it. What I mean by that is that researchers obtain the results, publish them, and feel like their job is done. But that is not enough for patients. Of course, they will be happy to know that the results were published but what they really look for is to understand how these results will impact patients' lives. So we need to push researchers to go this extra mile that they usually neglect. What I tell them is that if they request patients to fill out their surveys, they have a responsibility to provide them with the results. It's a win-win principle. You cannot ask for something and never give back or wait for years and years before publishing results. So, what I do now is that before recruiting patients for a survey, I ask researchers if they have enough resources to go through with their study and return results to patients. In addition, in upcoming years we would like to go as far as telling our researchers that if they don't make use of the data within two years after it was collected, we are allowed to take it back and use it ourselves. We find it unethical for patients to share their data, which I believe belongs to them, and never receive anything in return.

At the end of each study, participants have the opportunity to meet and interact with researchers. The study results are made available, and participants can ask all their questions. Guillemette Jacob told us that with this system in place, patients feel like they contribute to the greater good and are happy to be informed of the impact their participation has had on the medical field.

Research organizations across the globe are now developing ways to return results to patients. Part of this is due to clinical data transparency strategy that has been implemented in many organizations where the participant's data is made available to them.

Notes

1 European Union. Attitudes towards the impact of digitalization on daily lives, https://europa.eu/eurobarometer/surveys/detail/2228 (accessed August 2021).

2 Kalkman S, van Delden J, Banerjee A, et al. Patients' and public views and attitudes towards the sharing of health data for research: a narrative review of the empirical evidence. *J Med Ethics*. Published Online First: 12 November 2019. doi:10.1136/medethics-2019-105651

3 Goodman D, Johnson CO, Bowen D, et al. De-identified genomic data sharing: the research participant perspective. *J Community Genet*. 2017;8(3):173–181. doi:10.1007/s12687-017-0300-1

4 McCormick N, Hamilton CB, Koehn CL, et al. Canadians' views on the use of routinely collected data in health research: a patient-oriented cross-sectional survey. *CMAJ Open*. 2019;7(2):E203–E209. doi:10.9778/cmajo.20180105

5 NICE Citizens Council, What Ethical and Practical Issues Need to Be Considered in the Use of Anonymized Information Derived from Personal Care Records as Part of the Evaluation of Treatments and Delivery of Care? London: National Institute for Health and Care Excellence (NICE); 11 November 2015.

6 Hill EM, Turner EL, Martin RM, et al. "Let's get the best quality research we can": public awareness and acceptance of consent to use existing data in health research: a systematic review and qualitative study. *BMC Med Res Methodol.* 2013;13(1):72. doi:10.1186/1471-2288-13-72

7 Kalkman S, van Delden J, Banerjee A, et al. Patients' and public views and attitudes towards the sharing of health data for research: a narrative review of the empirical evidence. *J Med Ethics.* Published Online First: 12 November 2019. doi:10.1136/medethics-2019-105651

8 Patil S, Lu H, Saunders CL, et al. Public preferences for electronic health data storage, access, and sharing – evidence from a pan-European survey. *J Am Med Inform Assoc.* 2016;23(6):1096–1106. doi:10.1093/jamia/ocw012

9 Sipilä J. Patients in Finland blackmailed after therapy records were stolen by hackers, *CNN Business*, https://edition.cnn.com/2020/10/27/tech/finland-therapy-patients-blackmailed-data-breach-intl/index.html (accessed August 2021).

10 Data Saves Lives. Public opinions and behaviour around health data in the GDPR era, https://datasaveslives.eu/public-opiniongdpr (accessed August 2021).

11 Moore S. Gartner predicts for the future of privacy 2020, *Gartner*, https://www.gartner.com/smarterwithgartner/gartner-predicts-for-the-future-of-privacy-2020/ (accessed August 2021).

12 Dao T. Who owns patients' data? *Pharmacy Times*, https://www.pharmacytimes.com/view/who-owns-patients-data (accessed August 2021).

13 Carter P, Laurie GT, Dixon-Woods M. The social licence for research: why care.data ran into trouble. *J Med Ethics.* 2015;41:404–409.

14 Triggle N. Care.data: how did it go so wrong? *BBC*, https://www.bbc.com/news/health-26259101 (accessed August 2021).

15 Richter G, Borzikowsky C, Lieb W, et al. Patient views on research use of clinical data without consent: legal, but also acceptable? *Eur J Hum Genet.* 2019;27:841–847. doi:10.1038/s41431-019-0340-6

Chapter 4

Applications of Health Data

Health data includes any patient's data captured either digitally or on paper. In order to have the best benefit, all health data needs to be digital format in order to analyze the information for the different applications or use to benefit the patients (the ultimate stakeholder). Many countries have started the painful transition of moving the citizen's health data to electronic. These technologies that can transmit and receive electronic health data are referred to as digital health. It includes technologies like mobile health (mHealth), platforms, and systems that engage consumers for lifestyle, wellness, health-related purposes, provide real-time monitoring of patient's vital signs, collect digital social and behavioural information including patient reported data, deliver information to care providers and/or researchers, and/or support life science and clinical operations. It can also directly or indirectly monitor or enhance health or coordinate healthcare services.

In 2009, we saw a push of digitalization of medical records in the United States. Data from the US Department of Health and Human Services show that in 2017, 96% of hospitals and

DOI:10.4324/9781003215868-4

86% of physicians' offices in the United States had access to electronic health records.[1]

Kaiser Family Foundation (KFF) is a non-profit organization focusing on national health issues, as well as the US role in global health policy, conducted a poll in 2019 on the public's experience with electronic health records. It found that, for example, a majority (57%) of adults aged 18–29 say that the quality of care they receive is "better", while none say that it is "worse", as a result of their physician using a computer-based medical record. In addition, 45% report feeling "very concerned" or "somewhat concerned" that there are errors in their personal health information that may negatively affect their care. While nearly half of those with EHRs are concerned about errors in their records (40% of total), one in five say that they or a family member have noticed an error in their EHR. The most-reported errors are incorrect medical history (9%); fewer report incorrect personal information (5%), incorrect lab or test results (3%), incorrect medication or prescription information (3%), and billing issues (less than 1%).[2]

This chapter explores ways in which patient registries, research, and national health systems may be able to take advantage of digital health technologies, with a particular focus on the strengths and limitations of these technologies to collect patient-generated health data, a discussion on how they are currently being used, and the anticipated value that it will bring to the three main areas: patients, society, and researchers.

Applications of Health Data

Why Is It Important?

The cost of healthcare has increased over the years (refer to Chapter 2). In the UK, NHS (National Health System) invests 25% of the central government. Funding for health services in

England comes from the Department for Health and Social Care's budget. Planned spending for the Department of Health and Social Care in England was £212.1 billion in 2020/21, up from £150.4 billion in 2019/20. This includes more than £60 billion of extra funding for the Department of Health and Social Care 2020/21 in response to the Covid-19 pandemic. Budgets rose by 1.4 per cent each year on average (adjusting for inflation) in the 10 years between 2009/10 to 2018/19.[3]

According to a US poll from KFF in 2019, the majority of the uninsured are putting off care due to cost and 25% of the responders said that their condition got worse as a result.[4] The cost of healthcare and treatments are preventing access to people who are most in need. This is eroding our society and creating wider disparity. Therefore, reducing health equity. People are not treated right away or getting the right care will ultimately result in higher costs for healthcare whether they have insurance or not, whether the healthcare is paid privately or publicly (via the government).

It is important to state that despite the issues on data access, having the right data, data diversity, and unbiased data, we need to be creative and find ways to make data interoperable. Also, we need to have robust processes to manage the power of data as explained in Chapter 3 (big data). Christian et al.[5] explains that the advances in technology and computational sophistication will provide advances in healthcare. They split this into four quadrants: 1) Diagnostics (e.g. point-of-care diagnostics); 2) Treatment (e.g. telehealth services); 3) Public health (e.g. disease and health surveillance); and 4) Research (e.g. remote or decentralized clinical trials). Social media's impact in healthcare has also significantly grown and while there have been increases in published research using social media, benefits are not clear, and policies still need to be put in place. Despite all of this growth in digital health, the collective understanding of how these components, devices, and technologies work still remains fragmented and data is still disparate.

While many experts in the field categorizes the use and applications differently, we categorize them in three main areas based on the stakeholders:

1. Researcher: opportunities to advance drug development, targeted, and best treatment and care.
2. Society: opportunities to improve healthcare for the common good or society including prevention of infectious diseases.
3. Citizen: opportunities for citizens to be informed, better manage their health and care by choosing the best or right treatment and health services.

Many of the applications are based on data analysis to more sophisticated solutions like artificial intelligence. As explained in Chapter 3, data analytics have supported many applications but there are other opportunities that have not being explored yet. It's not because there is no interest, rather it requires investment, data to be accessible and interoperable, skilled resources to bring the data together that can be ingested and analyzed. The application of big data analytics in healthcare has a lot of positive and also life-saving outcomes. Applied to healthcare, it will use specific health data of a population (or of a particular individual) and potentially help to prevent epidemics, cure disease, improve healthcare, etc. The recent development of artificial intelligence (AI), machine learning, image processing, and data mining techniques are helping data scientists to use the big data in healthcare in a centric approach. This helps finding patterns and making visual representation on the health data for different purposes and use.

The years of gathering huge amounts of data for medical use has been costly and time-consuming. But with the constant enhancements of technologies, it has become easier to collect, report, and convert them into relevant critical insights that can then be used to provide better treatment and care. The healthcare data analytics will help to find, predict, and solve problems faster, involving patients more in their own health and ultimately empower them to use the right tools that will ultimately benefit them. The applications in Figure 4.1 are potential uses of the health data if made available, with the right permissions, unbiased, and linked, mapped, or integrated with a robust IT and Data governance in place. Therefore, let's get started with a list of usages and examples of big data and data science in healthcare.

Researcher

A researcher in healthcare or clinical carries out academic or scientific research. The purpose of their role is to study the illnesses in people. In addition to discover new ways to treat the disease, how to prevent and diagnose. Figure 4.2 shows the various applications in health data that researchers could benefit from. In this section, we will explain some of the applications and the impact that it has in healthcare and drug development.

Disease Identification and Diagnosis

Clinical researchers use genomics data, imaging, medical history, and family medical history to identify patterns and support the early diagnosis of for example a hereditarian condition. It also can help to predict the disease progression of the patients. With more data shared by citizens and patients, data analytics can play a pivotal role in the development of ground-breaking new drugs and forward-thinking therapies.

For example, find the best treatment for cancer patients using a large amounts of patient data on their treatment plans

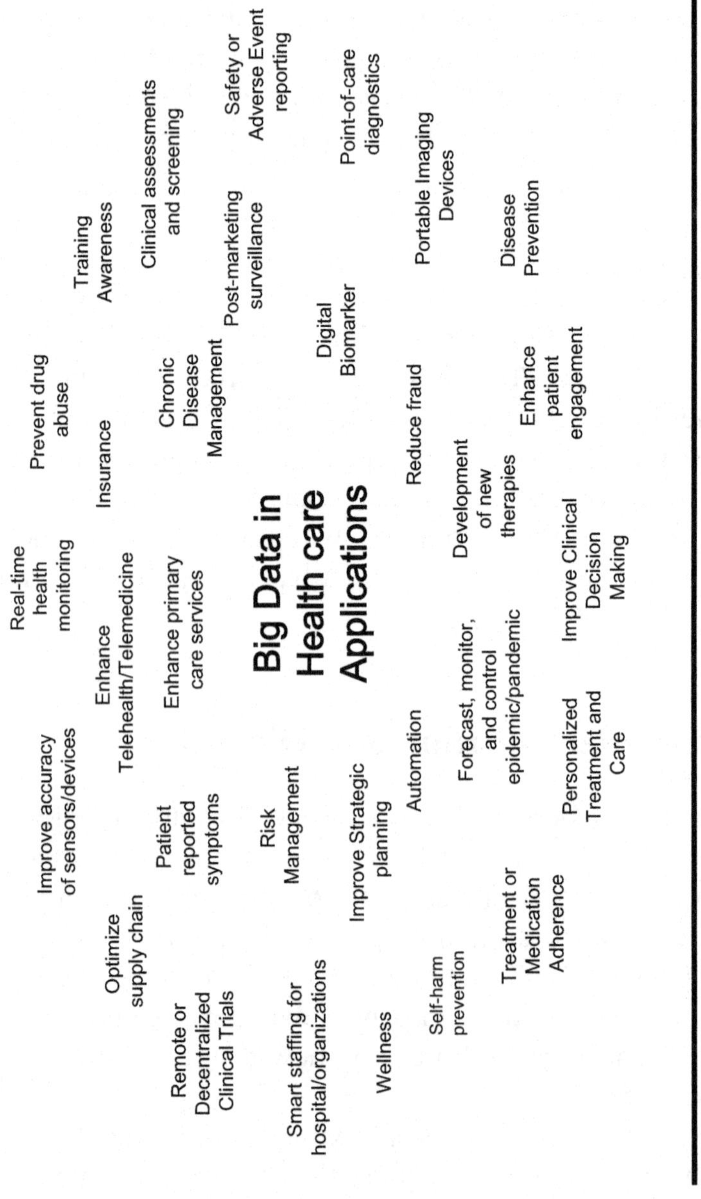

Figure 4.1 Big data applications.

Figure 4.2 Research applications.

and recovery rates. In addition, researchers could find trends and mutations based on how treatments might affect cancer proteins using the tumour samples in biobanks, linking to patient treatment.

Digital Therapeutics

Digital therapeutic targets specific clinical outcomes in line with the defined clinical indication and patient population. They are scientifically validated apps and devices. Usually are prescribed by a doctor often alongside a medicine to deliver software generated therapeutic interventions with the aim to improve patient's health.

For example, digital therapeutics can include gamification to treat mental and behavioural health issues. Another example is lung rehabilitation and predicting heart failure by monitoring patients' symptoms and vital signs using complex mathematical rules and calculations (algorithms), it can alert a physician as to how well the patient is doing on the treatment, to maximize both safety and outcomes. All these require patient data to validate the apps and devices, and the ability to analyse big quantities of data to ensure measurements are clinical standards.

Personalized Treatment

Personalized treatments include precision medicine which helps with selecting and tailoring the treatment for individual patients using genetic, environmental, and lifestyle information. It also includes gene therapy which is the closest thing in finding a cure for the patient's condition. The high cost of personalized treatment is due to the manufacturing or production of a single drug specific to an individual, making it not accessible to all the patient population. But when looking at a chronic condition where patients might live with the disease for decades, the cost of personalized treatment might be a better option comparable to the cost of drug treatment, cost of care, and quality of life. For example, cystic fibrosis gene therapy is available, but treatments are expensive, costing around US $1 million per patient. Also, only an estimated 10% of patients will not be responsive to these classes of drugs due to gene mutations. These types of gene editing would provide a one-time cure without the need for continuous expensive therapies and would be cheaper than continuous drug therapy which costs around US$250,000 per year per patient.[6]

Drug Discovery

Researchers are able to predict initial screening of drug compounds using machine learning to analyse the success rate on the drug efficacy and safety based on biological elements. In addition, to also understand any secondary use of drug, different disease, or condition, using simulation to predict whether the drug could target the specific biological entity.

As an example, big data has supported novel anti-cancer drug discovery. In an article by Bernstead-Hume et al.,[7] they discuss the use of analysis of genomic sequencing data, pathway data, multi-platform data, identifying genetic interactions such as deficiencies in the expression of two or more genes leads to cell death and using cell line data. Also, they looked at the patterns of mutations within driver genes enable identification of genes into oncogenes (gene that can transform a cell into tumour cell) and tumour suppressors (anti-oncogenes). Tumour suppressors cannot often be directly targeted. Instead, analysis is required to find gene products that are synthetically lethal to the tumour suppressor and can be inhibited pharmacologically. The genetic dependencies of cancer cell lines can be profiled, identifying where the cancer has become addicted to support from altered pathways, allowing new therapeutic options. Analysis of omics (e.g. genomics, proteomics, metagenomics) data from cell lines tested with novel compounds has allowed genetic, lineage, and gene-expression-based predictors of drug sensitivity.

The use of secondary data or reuse of data is related to reuse of clinical data for a different purpose than the one for which it was originally collected. The data being reused are usually anonymized and owned by e.g. hospitals and health systems. It includes claims and patient health data. This data is usually reused for research, patient safety, and improve quality of care and services.

Clinical Trials

Using health data to identify the right participants for the clinical trial based on their demographic and medical history. It can lead to accelerating the drug development process as recruitment takes approximately one-third of the clinical trial. New medicines can be made available sooner than the 10–12 years that it takes.

Another example is the in-silico trials. This is still in its beginning but consists of using patient data to predict how an individual patient will respond to certain conditions, predict the outcome of the research based on the compound, population, and criteria. It is a computer simulated clinical trial. These digital trials can improve the design of a clinical trial involving patients, provide an early estimate of efficacy over large, simulated cohorts or patient population, etc. The same can be applied for pre-clinical data, animal data.

Also, US FDA are providing guidance on how to use simulations to accelerate the progress of drugs to market, such as in the safety of vaccines for children also modelling and simulation to support dose selection and/or study design, data analysis, and interpretation for planned paediatric studies.[8]

For patient-specific computer models, computer models of disease progression and treatment response can represent each physical individual (digital twin) or a hypothetical individual whose key characteristics (described by the inputs of the model) are sampled from the joint distribution of a representative population (digital trials).

Two other examples from an expert working in a pharmaceutical company are: 1) Using clinical trial data to inform pre-clinical data to understand mouse data. Using information from clinical data or even real-world data (RWD) to be able to inform how pre-clinical data could be interpreted better, which would help researchers to interpret and better predict future clinical trial design and outcome; and 2) Use of tokens or tokenization (based on methods from cryptography and discrete mathematics) by which we can connect data about patients in different RWD sources without compromising their rights to privacy. Therefore, the patient's prescription information, medical records, and insurance information could all be combined into a single view, for example, who they are as a patient, what are their patterns of care consumption, the impact on treatments and adherence, which outcomes the patient wants to achieve, and how it impacts your clinical outcomes.

Use of clinical trial data with the RWD can be used to simulate the efficacy and safety of the medicine. A recent study used RWD from a Phase 3 clinical data to simulate the safety of the medicine in Alzheimer's patient population. They used two main scenarios: 1) A one-treatment simulation using a standard-of-care (SOC) that can serve as an external control arm; and 2) A two-treatment simulation using both intervention and control treatments with proper patient matching algorithms for comparative effectiveness analysis. It was observed that the second scenario had higher serious adverse event (SAE) rates in the simulated trials than the rates reported in original trial, and a higher SAE rate was observed in medicine treatment than in the SOC treatment. In the first scenario, similar estimates of SAE rates were observed when proportional sampling was used to control demographic variables. This type of trial simulation using RWD is feasible in this example. Trial simulation using RWD is a valuable tool for post-market comparative effectiveness studies and for informing future trials' design.[9]

In our interview with Gloria Kayani, Chief Operating Officer for TRI (Thrombosis Research Institute), she mentioned that the ideal future is breaking the big barrier of bypassing clinicians and going directly to the patients. As an example, in the context of clinical research (observational study), arming patients with good data, medical history, and behaviour data where information is not abused, researchers can work with empowered patients. This completely removes clinicians, and patients work directly with the researchers. If we are only collecting data, why do we need an investigative site to do that if it's not intrusive and not an interventional study? If I am educated (health-literate), I can work with researchers without going to GPs and clinicians, and even be compensated; there is incentive to sell my data: why should doctors get paid if it's a simple transfer of data?

Comorbidities

Simulation of how a medicine might react to other comorbidities is important and should be further explored. Clinical trials design tends to be specific to only invite participants who have one disease. The reality is that according to Adams et al.,[10] 45.4% of adults reported at least one of the comorbidities, cardiovascular disease, chronic obstructive pulmonary disease (COPD), diabetes, asthma, hypertension, and/or cancer other than skin. The researchers used 2017 Behavioural Risk Factor Surveillance System (BRFSS) data. Starting from 19.8% for ages 18–29 years to 80.7% for ages 80+ years. Rates also varied by race/ethnicity, health insurance status, and employment. Based on these types of simulations with RWD and Clinical Trial data we will be able to predict how the medicine could react to the other comorbidities, interact with other drugs, evaluate the efficacy, and safety of the medication.

Society (Healthcare System)

Healthcare systems are responsible for delivering services that improve, maintain or restore the health of individuals and their communities. It includes prevention and control disease, promoting health, health planning, and improving the social, economic, or environmental conditions in which people live. Health systems are also responsible for the careful management (or stewardship) of these services to ensure that they reach everyone equally, are responsive to individual needs and vulnerabilities.[11] Figure 4.3 shows some of these applications that benefits the communities when data is shared and used for the greater good of the society.

Hospital Performance, Planning and Management

Every year, many patients die due to the unavailability of a doctor at the most critical time. Using health data and historical hospital records will predict, for example, the number of patients that will be seen at the hospital, number of beds available, and number of staff available during critical times. This will help to focus on reducing the waiting time for patients and extending the quality of healthcare services.

Figure 4.3 Society and healthcare applications.

Through utilization of key performance indicators and data analytics, the hospitals are able to track and monitor in real time (e.g. average hospital stay, medical equipment utilization, treatment cost, patient room turnover rate, patient wait time, patient satisfaction, patient safety). This application is not only for hospital administrators but also important for doctors to improve the overall patient's care. Also, to reduce health inequalities especially with availability of specialist doctors in rural vs. urban areas, increase hospital performance and access to care and improve management of these. Moreover, data analysis will empower senior staff to improve strategic planning and make vital staff and personnel management processes as efficient as possible. For example, Intel and the Assistance Publique-Hôpitaux de Paris (AP-HP), the largest university hospital in Europe, developed a cloud-based solution for predicting the expected number of patient visits and hospital admissions using advanced data science methodologies. They used data from four emergency departments within AP-HP. Although it is only a prototype, it will enable the hospital administrators to view predictions of emergency department visits and hospital admissions to optimize staffing levels based on anticipated needs.[12]

In addition, using health data will help hospitals and clinics to maintain a good supply chain to support patient care and treatment, making it efficient from end to end, leveraging analytics tools to track the supply chain performance metrics, and make accurate, data-driven decisions concerning operations as well as spending can save hospitals millions of dollars per year.

The use of dashboards will provide a big picture of the hospital or facility and empower the users and decision makers to act quick and improve on future planning. For example, having the trends week by week on numbers of outpatients vs. inpatients, total number of admissions, number of patients by department or division, patient satisfaction, average waiting time in emergency rooms, number of available beds, etc. will help identify any potential bottlenecks, trends, and provide an overview of the overall operations.

Another real-world application is to visualize service levels and treatment accuracy across departments including the percentage of equipment utilization, cost of drug per patient, bed occupancy rate. These metrics will help project the number of staff needed at a certain time and streamlining care processes across departments leading to cost savings.

Pandemic and Epidemic

Using a predictive model that forecasts how the upcoming season for cold and flu would affect different regions, and when are the predicted peaks and troughs. The advantage of this information is to inform citizens, improve our national and regional healthcare delivery system, and timing (distribution, stock up, display, and secondary support).

Covid-19 pandemic projections have been very helpful for the government to make decisions to safeguard citizens' health and prevent more deaths. The Institute for Health Metrics and Evaluation collaborates with various partners. Their projections show both reported deaths, which is the number of deaths officially reported as Covid-19, and excess deaths related to Covid-19, which is all deaths estimated as attributed to Covid-19, including unreported deaths. Estimating the excess Covid-19 death rate is important both for modelling the transmission dynamics of the disease to make better forecasts, and for understanding the drivers of larger and smaller epidemics across different countries. Their projection contains summaries of the results for more than 230 locations, and special analyses.[13] These types of projects are life-saving, and it is for the greater good of society. It has helped governments to make informed decisions on when to exercise lockdown either national or regional level, the length of lockdowns, and communicate and educate the population to take precautionary measures to avoid transmission from one person to another.

Improving Medical or Healthcare Services

Some examples of using data analytics are to improve medical services and use data analytics to identify symptoms. Using data collected from patients, physicians can check if the condition of any patient is healthy, see any trends and patterns that might require diagnosis, and advise the best course of treatment or services. Also, to prevent patients being re-tested if they have already carried out other tests at other hospitals.

Another area that big data is tackling is mental health. According to WHO, suicide is a global phenomenon: 77% of suicides occurred in low- and middle-income countries in 2019. Suicide accounted for 1.3% of all deaths worldwide, making it the 17th leading cause of death in 2019.[14] The Mental Health Research Network and Kaiser Permanente used EHR data, and a standard depression questionnaire identified individuals who had an enhanced risk of a suicide attempt with great accuracy. Utilizing a predictive algorithm, the team found that suicide attempts and successes were 200 times more likely among the top 1% of patients flagged according to specific datasets.[15] This type of predictive analytics will improve suicide prevention and help integrate care and coverage.

Substance Abuse

In the United States, the opioid crisis is a serious problem, which was responsible for most of the deaths in the US. It became necessary to tackle the problem of people using opioid drugs that include the illegal drug heroin, synthetic opioids, and pain relievers like oxycodone. Many initiatives started to solve the problem, but until the introduction of big data, the government and healthcare system were unable to detect patients who are at high risk and to start understanding the scale of the problem at hand.

Predictive modelling could transport the concept of stratified medicine to public health through novel methods, such as predictive modelling and emulated trials for evaluating diagnoses and prognoses of opioid use disorder, predicting treatment response, and providing targeted treatment recommendations. Surveillance systems play a crucial role in ensuring that agencies have the necessary information to be able to design, implement, and adapt public health interventions to ongoing problems and health harms efficiently and effectively.[16]

The data collected is a blend from medical history, insurance companies, and pharmacies. Using predictive model to an accurate prediction of those with higher risks. It not only identifies patients who are abusing opioids but also reports to their physicians. This offers hope towards mitigating an issue which is destroying the lives of many people and creating higher costs for healthcare system.

Diagnosis Using Imaging Technologies

Diagnosis using imaging technologies are what radiologists do day by day. Sometimes, due to lack of availability of radiologist, there might be a delay on diagnosing a patient early while patient's health deteriorates or does not have the appropriate treatment that might make a difference. The application would be to replace images with numbers and perform algorithms for real-time assessment with accuracy. It would require storing medical images and working with radiologist to train the system (using AI and machine learning). This would undoubtedly impact the future role of radiologists, their education, and the required skillset.

NHSx is working in partnership with several government and NHS partners to deliver NHS AI Lab programmes and also provides funding to support projects that look to use AI to address the detection of disease and research into multiple long-term conditions. The NHSx, AI technologies applied to imaging, such as cancer screening, are among the most advanced uses of AI in healthcare. The AI Lab is supporting the development of imaging technology by setting up systems to safely collect and share data, making it easier to get new technologies into use in hospitals and care settings.[17]

Additionally, medical images are essential for generating metrics outcome and find specified patterns associated with the condition. It can increase the efficiency of the current radiologists to examine many more images and make comparisons.

Training Physicians and All Healthcare Providers

For institutions to run at an optimal capacity, it requires continuous training of staff from all levels, from porters, cleaners, and clerks to nurses and doctors. The importance is not only on the technical skills but also the soft skills.

Soft skills play an important part, for example having clear and effective communication with patients and work colleagues; improving critical thinking to analyzing information effectively and solve problems more quickly; and encouraging creativity in the workplace to enhance processes and procedures. The use of healthcare data analysis will help gain insight into who needs support or training. This could lead to higher patient satisfaction, improve quality of care and services, and cost savings for the institution.

Insurance

Big data in healthcare also includes claims data (insurance data). This is a rich source of information that includes information related to diagnoses, procedures, and utilization. There are numerous analyses that can be conducted on claims data to derive information and knowledge to drive decision-making. This information can be used for comparing prices of healthcare services at local, state, regional, or national levels. Also comparing services and quality of care provided by specific providers or healthcare organizations. Analytics help to streamline the processing of insurance claims, enabling patients to get better returns on their claims and caregivers are paid faster.

Another problem that big data and claims data can help is to tackle insurance fraud. According to the FBI (Federal Bureau of Investigation),[18] insurance fraud affects individuals and businesses alike, causing tens of billions of dollars in losses each year. It can raise health insurance premiums, expose citizens to unnecessary medical procedures, and increase taxes. Healthcare fraud can be committed by medical providers, patients, and others who intentionally deceive the healthcare system to receive unlawful benefits or payments. These include double billing, phantom billing, identity theft (of both patients and healthcare providers), fraud involving prescriptions like diverting legal prescriptions for illegal uses. Claims data can help health insurance companies to provide the best service and making it easy for them to detect any fraud activities. It can also prevent patient needing to pay for the same medical test several times.

Patient Engagement

Patient engagement is crucial to ensure patients remain active on their healthcare, have a shared decision-making about their health, and improving their health and wellbeing. These all depend on creating awareness, training, and improving communication from service providers to patients. In order for patients to take an active role in their own health, they must have a good understanding of their medical data and how to use that information to make more informed decisions. Complicated by medical jargon and low health literacy can lead to poor medication adherence, therefore, resulting in poor disease management. The other problem is the lack of trust in healthcare and pharmaceutical industries and the rise in health service costs. Therefore, it is important to support global initiatives that supports patient awareness and training to increase their health literacy, digital literacy, and understanding of clinical trials and research.

Health data can help build patient engagement tools that target specific areas or diseases. For example, patients with chronic diseases can benefit with self-management interventions allowing patients to independently keep track of their health and actively engage in their own care. This is vital to maintain their health and improve their quality of life.

We have seen an increase on mHealth and use of health apps including devices and wearables or data aggregations to supplement their healthcare. If we aggregated data that consists of demographics, medical conditions, compliance, and treatment outcomes, it could provide insight into what programmes may help specific patients and which are at risk for non-compliance.

Citizen (Patients)

A patient receives medical care and treatment from healthcare providers. There are many advantages for patients that only more recently have started to emerge. As described in Chapter 1, the rise of patient empowerment, the need to be involved at every step in decisions related to their health. But most importantly is to trust the system and understand the benefits in order to be more engaged about their health and access of health information. Figure 4.4 provides a list of applications that would benefit the citizens or patients. This list is not exhaustive, as advances in science and technology continues to evolve, so will be future needs for patients.

Improve Disease Management, Quality of Life, Health, and Wellness

We are living in the age of information. Data in science and healthcare is a most valuable asset. This application uses big data to outline a personalized treatment plan, improve quality of life, wellness plan including nutrition plan for people who suffers from various diseases. The data would come from different sources, not only from medical information, apps, wearables, devices but also social media, and browser history. All these data can tailor a specific plan for an individual to improve overall health and wellness.

With the use of IoT devices, access to their health data in an aggregated manner including real-time alerts are ways to help patients to be more engaged and manage their condition. But not all solutions are without issues. The issues are integrating data from various sources to have a meaningful aggregated view of your health and that's easy to interpret. Other issues are that not all devices are fit for purpose, and not one device is able to measure or track all symptoms per condition. Also, issues around data integrity and quality: what if you have two devices that measure heart rate, but there are discrepancies between them; which data should be used?

Aside from using IoT devices, with patients' health data, the doctors' data-centric approach for treating patients with

Figure 4.4 Patient applications.

no or minimal margin for error involves observing their lifestyle and bringing changes to their health, like patients who are suffering from high blood pressure, asthma, etc. This is a way of personalizing what's important for the individual. Using a platform that collects and organizes data from laboratory reports, clinical notes, radiology scans, and pathology images helps physicians make more personalized and informed treatment plans.

In terms of wellness and nutrition plans, we can use big data to unlock thousands of possibilities that can support patients. From collecting data from wearables such heart rate, movement, food e-diary, and other health apps to gather insights for nutrition and wellbeing. This application observes the daily life, food habits, and behaviour of people to help them to have a healthier lifestyle, including physical and mental wellbeing.

Preventing Medication or Treatment Errors

Medication management is complex, involving multiple people and numerous steps. Medication errors are mistakes either in the prescribing, dispensing, or administration of medicinal products. The most common (although preventable) errors are wrong drugs, method of administration, dose, and treatment to the wrong patient.

The European Patients' Forum[19] mentions that in Europe, 7.5% of medication errors occur at the prescription stage and 0.08% at the dispensing stage, while in hospitals, medication errors represent 18.7–56% of all adverse drug events among patients. Patients also make mistakes while using medications. The annual cost of medication errors is estimated between €4.5 billion and €21.8 billion.

Dialogue between patients and healthcare professionals is key. Healthcare professionals often overestimate the quality of the information they provide, whereas patients would like to know more. Patients can help prevent errors and be active members of their healthcare team. Patients' access to their own medical record is of paramount importance and the cornerstone of empowerment. It would also enable patients and their caregivers to correct errors in the record. Firstly, patients need access to their health records, unfortunately, this is not always the case. In addition, there needs to be patient friendly information or in plain language on the medication that is being prescribed. Patients need to inform and remind doctors of their allergies and previous side effects using a particular treatment or drug, other medication that they are taking to ensure that there a no contraindications. Patients should ask questions to gain more understanding of their medicine, ask the pharmacist how to take the medication before or after food, can you drink alcohol, what are the side effects, etc.

Although patients can help improve safety, the improvement of medication safety as a whole needs to involve all stakeholders and patient organizations as well as healthcare professionals, regulatory bodies, and the industry.

Early Diagnosis of Potential Disease

With the use of patient data, doctors would be able to analyse earlier on any signs of conditions and provide an early diagnosis. Data analytics is key for preventive and predictive medicine. Many robust early detection services and other health-related technologies have developed from clinical and diagnostic evidence in both the data mining type of companies and healthcare providers. Machine learning and AI are commonly used in the research and healthcare sectors. These involve collecting and analyzing patient data with remote monitoring devices that includes diagnostic tools.

This helps to accelerate diagnoses and disease predictions, augment doctors or researchers' decision-making, deliver diagnostic insights to help clinicians make faster and more accurate diagnoses, and provide continuous care to patients.

For example, consider the Mayo Clinic developing and commercializing AI-enabled algorithms for early detection of conditions like a weak heart pump, silent arrhythmias, or a thickened heart pump before they pose a risk to developing stroke or heart failure. They use clinical data analytics platforms, including raw electrocardiogram (ECG) signals, to unlock hidden biomedical knowledge and enable early detection as well as accelerate treatment of heart disease. One research was ECG AI-Guided Screening for Low Ejection Fraction (EAGLE). It aimed at determining whether an AI-enabled ECG algorithm trial could help improve the diagnosis of this condition. It detected patients with low ejection fraction. This is a measurement of how much blood the left ventricle pumps out with each contraction. A lower-than-normal ejection fraction can be a sign of heart failure.[20] Early diagnosis can be key to effective treatment. AI cardiology allows doctors to spend more time with their patients and improves the shared decision-making process. Preventing heart problems and detecting failures sooner.

Reduce and Prevent Fraud

In the previous section, we discussed insurance fraud within the healthcare system. It also uses claims data and health data to be able to detect fraudulent activity. This application is using data science to protect the data from many patients from criminals who steals the data and sells it in the black market. For patients, the risk is very high due to the sensitivity of the data: Personal Health Information (PHI) which makes patients identifiable. It contains not only their medical information and history, but possibly also family history.

Dealing with false claims is a serious problem. The use of data analytics can successfully detect fraud claims and enables insurance companies to provide better returns on the real patients. It can produce reliable detection of inaccurate claims and saves a lot of money for the insurance companies every year. It can avoid hassle for patients who had their identity and data stolen.

Insurance companies or payers need both visualization and predictive analytics tools to learn about providers with history of fraud and abuse, patterns related to overpaid claims, and where these activities are emerging from.

Fighting fraud protects consumers from overbilling, increased premiums, and ensures that financial assets are secure from criminal activity.

Patient Engagement

Patient engagement is about not only using for example devices and wearables, but also understanding their health and be an active participant on decision-making of their health and wellness. As per previous section, and Chapter 1, it concerns establishing trust in the healthcare team, support system, and the overall health ecosystem where patients come first. It is about showing the benefits for the patients when they shared their data, and how it can impact their lives. In a system where trust is established, engagement tends to be higher, and patients play a more active role, effectively becoming part of the health team.

A direct patient engagement is using the apps and devices that monitors the patient's health. Many consumers have an interest in smart devices that record for example their movement, heart rates, sleeping habits, and blood pressure on a continuous way. All these vital signs information and others can be aggregated with other device data to identify potential health risks for patients. For example, elevated blood pressure can be a signal of hypertension, or a high heart rate could indicate a future risk of heart disease. These type of alerts and indications will signal the patient to reach out to their healthcare providers to perform further tests to assess their health. Also, there are some specific devices where data is stored in cloud and accessible to their physicians, this allows them to track and monitor their health in real time. This reduces the necessity to visit the doctors frequently and also provides alerts if something is out of ordinary.

Patients who are already involved in the monitoring of their own health, health insurance companies have provided incentives for them to improve their health and to keep maintaining it. They either providing points to collect services at later stage or devices like smartwatch that further helps patients to monitor in an ongoing basis their vitals.

How to Create Incentives for Patients to Share Data

As healthcare costs continue to rise, insurance companies have invented ways to incentivize and motivate people to maintain their health. As we have seen in previous examples, the earlier the diagnosis, the less costly it will be for the patients in terms of insurance, and healthcare. Many insurance companies are switching from fee-for-service plans (for large patient population) to plans that tailored to patients' benefit.

Some have argued that financial incentives matter especially if they achieve personal goals. As many big companies who are data controllers and aggregators of information, they are for-profit organizations who understand the value of patient data. Similarly for healthcare providers, there is a direct incentive to share or sell patient information (anonymized or pseudo-anonymized) with one another, mainly used for research purposes. The argument that we have seen in previous chapters and in discussions with various interviewees for this book, is that if institutions are making money selling their data, why can't they also be remunerated for their contribution? After all, patients pay for the health services provided by their doctors, caregivers, or indirectly via taxes to the government. Likewise, some researchers also argue that by paying patients for their data might create data bias.

Regardless, if you lean towards patients getting paid or not, incentives are needed for patients to share their data. Incentives can be monetary or for the benefit of getting the best available or personalized treatment and better patient outcome. Physician decisions are becoming more and more evidence-based, they rely on research and clinical data. If more people's data is shared, it might lead to better outcomes for patients in general.

For incentives that are of monetary value, there are solutions like using points system, tokenization including non-fungible tokens (NFT), and cash. Point systems and tokenization can lead to trading or buying services, treatment, discounts, and free gifts.

MINI CASE STUDY 4.1:   NHS (UK)

The UK Health Data Research Alliance unifies leading healthcare and research organizations to establish best practice for the ethical use of UK health data for research at scale. They are the alliance of health data custodians. Their objective is to support the acceleration of health and care by encouraging widespread and responsible access to structured and unstructured clinical, administrative, imaging, genomic and other molecular data, in other words, patient data. The challenge is that only a fraction of the NHS data and research data is accessible. This makes it difficult to realize the full potential and value of the data, for example in diagnosis, prevention, and healthcare policies.[21] But there is always a question about the consent patients provided to the institution that is part of this alliance. Were patients aware that their pseudo-anonymized or anonymized data were being used? Are they aware of who is using it? Are they aware that their data is being sold to organizations for profit?

NHS Digital is the national custodian for health and care data in England and has responsibility for standardizing, collecting, analyzing, publishing and sharing data and information from across the health and social care system, including general practice. Their new system, General Practice Data for Planning and Research (GPDPR) was meant to roll out on the 1st of September 2021 with the intention to share patient data to support a wide variety of research and analysis to help run and improve health and care services. Patient data collected from general practice would be pseudo-anonymized and includes data on diagnoses, symptoms, observations, test results, medications, allergies, immunizations, referrals, recalls, and appointments, including information about physical, mental, and sexual health, data on sex, ethnicity, and sexual orientation, data about staff who have treated patients.[22] Although the intentions of why GPDPR was set up for is for the common good and to support patients, it was not transparent to all nor understood by all, especially what people consented for, and who will be allowed to access the data. GPDPR was put to a halt due to public outcry. The key problems were the lack of proper communication to the public and plan of how the data will be shared, and with whom would it be shared (organizations, institutions, etc.).

It raised many questions about data security, whether data could be identifying the person. That lack of transparency and clarification to the public, including the failure to involve and engage with wider community, resulted in distrust on NHS Digital. There are clearly many lessons to be learned from this; also, the fact that many people consented to their GP, and the use of their data to support their health. The wider use of their information was not clear to the public, and the fact that people needed to opt-out, not knowing what they initially opted into. On top of this, people still struggle to access their own data. As a citizen, you need to request it, and it takes at least seven days to access only a portion of the data. So, how come *others* can access their information, but it is difficult to retrieve their *own* information? If you are a data controller company in a private sector and not able to produce the data you are entitled to (either because you paid for it directly or indirectly), it's very likely you won't use their services again.

The overall problems the Department of Health and Social Care (NHS) needs to target is instilling trust to citizens by:

1. Providing an easier way for people to access their health information;
2. Creating awareness campaigns (digital health) and increasing the digital and health literacy;
3. Communicating frequently and often about future plans and allowing for public to ask questions;
4. Showing that you have a secure system and long-lasting system and solution; and
5. Aligning within Department of Health and Social Care and other initiatives on the data custodian and usage (e.g. Digital NHS, UK HDRA), who and what data is being shared across different government

departments or organizations? Government organizations are quite complex for ordinary people to understand, it needs to transparent how information is shared across.

Based on the halt of GPDPR, they have paused the collection of data, to provide more time to engage with physicians, patients, health charities and others, and to strengthen the plan.

UK HRD published the 'Building trust in data access through public'[23] initiated by their Public Advisory Board (PAB) to gather information about patient and public involvement in the assessment of data access requests and monitoring of data use. The survey was conducted between February and March 2021. It revealed disparate approaches from full public involvement in decisions about data access to none. The survey revealed many missed opportunities to inform and involve the public about policies in relation to health data use. There was a lack of consistency in how data access requests are assessed and publicized. It was apparent that most information about data access procedures is produced for researchers, not for the public. This creates the distrust in the government. Unfortunately, this would affect the improvements that citizens are waiting for regarding health and social care. Without health data, it is like the blind leading the blind.

Notes

1 Hecht J. The future of electronic health records. *Nature.* 2019;573:S114–S116, doi:10.1038/d41586-019-02876-y (accessed August 29, 2021).
2 Muñana C, Kirzinger A, Brodie M. *Data Note: Public's Experiences with Electronic Health Records.* Kaiser Family

Foundation, https://www.kff.org/other/poll-finding/data-note-publics-experiences-with-electronic-health-records/# (accessed August 31, 2021).

3 The King's Fund. The Department of Health and Social Care's budget. The NHS budget and how it has changed, https://www.kingsfund.org.uk/projects/nhs-in-a-nutshell/nhs-budget (accessed August 31, 2021).

4 Kirzinger A, et al. "Data note: American's challenges with healthcare costs. KFF (Kaiser Family Foundation), https://www.kff.org/health-costs/issue-brief/data-note-americans-challenges-health-care-costs/ (accessed August 31, 2021).

5 Christian J, Dasgupta N, Jordan M, et al. Digital health and patient registries: today, tomorrow, and the future. In: Gliklich RE, Dreyer NA, Leavy MB et al. (editors). *21st Century Patient Registries: Registries for Evaluating Patient Outcomes: A User's Guide*: 3rd Edition, Addendum [Internet]. Rockville (MD): Agency for Healthcare Research and Quality (US); 2018 March 3, https://www.ncbi.nlm.nih.gov/books/NBK493822/ (accessed September 1, 2021).

6 Hodges CA, Conlon RA. Delivering on the promise of gene editing for cystic fibrosis. *Genes Dis.* 2018;6(2):97–108. doi:10.1016/j.gendis.2018.11.005 (accessed September 11, 2021).

7 Benstead-Hume G, Wooller SK, Pearl FMG. Big data' approaches for novel anti-cancer drug discovery. *Expert Opin Drug Discov.* 2017 June;12(6):599–609. doi:10.1080/17460441.2017.1319356. Epub 2017 May 2. PMID: 28462602.

8 USA Food and Drug Administration (FDA). Paediatric study plans: content of and process for submitting initial paediatric study plans and amended initial paediatric study plans guidance for industry version July 2020, https://www.fda.gov/media/86340/download (accessed September 12, 2021).

9 Chen Z, Zhang H, Guo Y, et al. Exploring the feasibility of using real-world data from a large clinical data research network to simulate clinical trials of Alzheimer's disease. *npj Digit Med.* 2021;4:84. doi:10.1038/s41746-021-00452-1 (accessed September 12, 2021).

10 Adams ML, Katz D, Grandpre J. Population based estimates of comorbidities affecting risk for complications from Covid-19 in the US. medRxiv 2020.03.30.20043919. doi:10.1101/2020.03.30.20043919 (accessed September 12, 2021).

11 World Health Organization (WHO) Europe. Health systems. Health topics, https://www.euro.who.int/en/health-topics/Health-systems/pages/health-systems (accessed September 12, 2021).

12 Ambert K, et al. White paper French hospital uses trusted analytics platform to predict emergency department visits and hospital admissions. Intel. French Hospital and Intel Predict ER Visits and Admissions (accessed September 12, 2021).

13 IHME. Estimation of excess mortality due to Covid-19, http://www.healthdata.org/special-analysis/estimation-excess-mortality-due-covid-19-and-scalars-reported-covid-19-deaths (accessed September 12, 2021).

14 World Health Organization (WHO). Suicide data. Mental health and substance use, https://www.who.int/teams/mental-health-and-substance-use/suicide-data (accessed September 12, 2021).

15 Kent J. EHR data fuels accurate predictive analytics for suicide risk. Analytics in Action News, https://healthitanalytics.com/news/ehr-data-fuels-accurate-predictive-analytics-for-suicide-risk (accessed September 12, 2021).

16 Bharat C, Hickman M, Barbieri S, Degenhardt L. Big data and predictive modelling for the opioid crisis: existing research and future potential. *The Lancet. Digit. Health*. 2021;3(6):e397–e407. doi:10.1016/S2589-7500(21)00058-3 (accessed September 12, 2021).

17 UK National Health System (NHS). AI in imaging: supporting the adoption of AI screening technologies. NHSx, https://www.nhsx.nhs.uk/ai-lab/ai-lab-programmes/ai-in-imaging/ (accessed September 12, 2021).

18 USA Federal Bureau of Investigation (FBI). Healthcare fraud, https://www.fbi.gov/scams-and-safety/common-scams-and-crimes/health-care-fraud (accessed September 19, 2021).

19 European Patients Forum (EPF). Informed patients can help prevent medication errors, https://www.eu-patient.eu/News/News-Archive/informed-patients-can-help-prevent-medication-errors/ (accessed September 19, 2021).

20 Jercich K. An artificial intelligence-enabled electrocardiogram helped identify patients with low ejection fraction who previously "would have slipped through the cracks", https://www.healthcareitnews.com/news/mayo-clinic-trial-signals-potential-ai-guided-heart-disease-detection (accessed September 19, 2021).

21 UK Health Data Research Alliance. About, https://ukhealthdata.org/about/ (accessed September 19, 2021).

22 NHS Digital. GP data for planning and research: letter from parliamentary under Secretary of State for Health and Social Care to general practices in England – 19 July 2021. General Practice Data for Planning and Research, https://digital.nhs.uk/data-and-information/data-collections-and-data-sets/data-collections/general-practice-data-for-planning-and-research/secretary-of-state-letter-to-general-practice (accessed September 19, 2021).

23 Health Data UK. Building trust in data access through public involvement in governance. Survey findings and recommendations from HDR UK's Public Advisory Board June 2021, https://www.hdruk.ac.uk/wp-content/uploads/2021/07/280621-PAB-Data-Access-procedures-paper-Building-trust-in-data-access-through-public-involvement-in-governance.pdf (accessed September 19, 2021).

Chapter 5

Data-Driven and Patient-Centred Health Systems

Across the globe, access to care and digital health services are unequal. This is due to socioeconomic and political factors, cultural barriers that lead to disenfranchized communities, and systemic racism. There is still a big gap that society needs to address and how to balance the access to healthcare for all populations. The high cost of healthcare and cost of living, creates a big divide between those who can afford better care vs. those living in the poverty line. The question is: Can technology and digitalization bridge those barriers? Maybe. While some countries are tech savvy and succeeded in conducting a systemic transformation of their health system, others struggle to move past their legacy systems and innovate. Depending on the nature of the health system, the relation to data can also drastically change. This observation has been emphasized during the Covid-19 pandemic when the capacity to collect, process, and understand data was essential to successfully navigate the events.

DOI:10.4324/9781003215868-5

In parallel, the health system in many countries is forced to evolve, driven by more active and engaged patients in their care. The growing number of patients suffering from chronic conditions pushes the system to rethink long-term care and patient education to reduce the impact of the disease on their quality of life. The rise of at-home care necessitates a strong relationship between health providers and patients to maintain an appropriate level of care outside the traditional setting of a hospital. Finally, the boom of e-patients, emphasized by access to information and digital solutions, needs to be met by the appropriate resources to co-construct the future of health services.

In this chapter, we will provide some examples of the digital strategies set up by different developed countries and their challenges.

Health Data Availability and Use across the World

As we discussed in this book, the healthcare industry has a large volume of data at its disposal but seems to struggle to make use of it. Despite economies all over the world investing a substantial percentage of their GDP in health, they only allocate an average of 5% of their health budgets to data management.[1] However, expenditure is not the only reason countries struggle with the digital transformation of their health industries. As an example, in 2017 the US spent over 17% of their GDP, whereas Finland spent only 9%. Yet, the Scandinavian country is considered among the most digitally advanced countries in the world. In fact, Finland started setting the basis of a national digital health strategy as early as 1995 and benefited from a strong political will aligned with appropriate resources and a culture for change. In contrast, the US reached a national digital health strategy 10 years later, in 2005. The World Health Organization points out in a 2016 report that the countries that developed their digital health strategies earlier on are now moving on to evaluation of their progress, adjusting their action plans and developing new services based on citizens' feedback. In Sweden, for instance, the focus has recently been shifting to a more balanced decision-making process between healthcare stakeholders and citizens and digital health co-development initiatives. The Covid-19 pandemic acted like a wakeup-call for all economies to make health data more available for the public and private sector while ensuring its appropriate and safe use.

OECD research suggests that the countries with the higher health data availability and use are Denmark, South Korea, Sweden, and Finland[2] (Figure 5.1). This assessment is based on several criteria: the number of key national datasets available, the population coverage of these datasets, the use of standard codes and unique ID or the automatic extraction of data from clinical or administrative records. Unsurprisingly, the Nordics are among the most advanced countries in terms of health data. As an example, Finland developed a national EHR system that allows health professionals to access a patient's

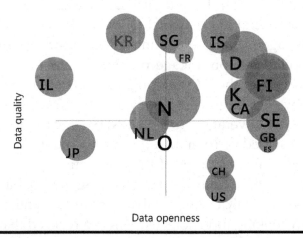

Figure 5.1 National databases in countries worldwide.

medical records at any time while also allowing researchers to extract data for their own work. These records are accessible to patients through a dedicated portal that also offers them additional digital health services such as prescription renewal or access control over their data. Moreover, Finland innovated by allowing patients to upload data from their apps and wearables directly into their web portal.

Most OECD countries have datasets that cover the entire population, which makes it easier to benefit from a comprehensive view of the health system and of public health. These datasets contain various types of data depending on the country and the nature of its health system: claims data, disease registries, in-patient data, prescriptions, etc. There are various reasons that explain why some countries might be lacking key datasets: the inability to connect all healthcare providers to an integrated or federated system, a decentralized healthcare system with regional management or datasets that by nature are samples of the population. In countries like the US, some datasets have gaps because they are missing data from private health providers. The UK, US, and Canada reported that more complete databases were available at sub-national levels. These countries often have their health systems organized at regional or federal levels, which impacts the way their health data is managed. In these circumstances, countries reported that they often rely on linkage projects to connect the different areas. In the UK, national datasets are managed centrally by NHS Digital, and they are therefore expected to have a greater coverage. However, NHS Digital only covers publicly provided or reimbursed services which can account for the poor representation of the population.

In other countries, the system was designed from a payer's perspective and only claims databases cover the entire population. Talking to various experts, we realized that most health systems are not designed for the purpose of sharing health data across various stakeholders and using it for purposes outside of care. Indeed, the main goal of health systems has always been to prove care to patients. Therefore, the first data collection processes were purely clinical and limited to the medical team. They included physician's notes, prescriptions, tests, etc. Then, economic considerations were added, and a new system had to be invented for payers. This is when administrative data emerged. As we can see, data collection and processing were created to serve immediate purposes and evolved as the healthcare system shifted and uncovered new needs. Unfortunately, there is little anticipation of upcoming transformations and therefore, health systems struggle to adapt. As an example, given to us during interviews, health systems today make very little use of real-world data. As thoroughly discussed in previous chapters, real-world data is crucial to understand patient outcomes in their everyday lives, monitor the performance of the health system and manage public health policies. However, the conditions to make the most of this type of data are not met in most countries: standards are challenging to implement, data collection is slowed down by constraining regulations, governance is unclear and fragmented, and overall, there is no unified strategy at national levels. Consequently, health systems fail to adapt to new demands and are stuck in legacy systems.

Nevertheless, there are a few examples of initiatives that show that some countries can respond to new needs when and adapt their health data collection to new purposes.

The Swedish National Diabetes Register

In 1996, Sweden created the Swedish National Diabetes Register (NDR) to help clinicians across the country measure their clinical performance and compare it to the national average.[3] The long-term goal was to reduce diabetes mortality and morbidity but also to identify the most cost-effective care.

In 2014, the NDR created the Button tool, which made online data available to everyone.[4] It allows researchers, physicians, and anyone interested to navigate the dataset and see how well different health facilities meet their targets. As data is available down to the health centre, public authorities are enabled to better manage discrepancies in the quality of care and allocate resources more precisely.

It is noteworthy that patients have an important role in the registry's steering group and are part of every decision-making process. One of their main focuses at the moment is to allow all patients to see their data directly. In this context, the Button received wide support as it provided patient association with data that they were able to use in advocacy efforts.

Israel: Data vs. Vaccine

Israel is known as one of the most advanced digital health systems in the world and a recognized innovation hub. Its citizens are all affiliated to one of the four health insurance providers that also include most of the country's hospitals and health professionals. Israel developed a single EHR system that is accessible to all citizens and health providers, independently of the insurance they work with. As a result, the country has a comprehensive health database of approximately 9 million citizens. In 2018, Israel allocated $300 million to develop this large database and make it accessible to researchers, medical teams or entrepreneurs.[5]

The country drew attention during the Covid-19 pandemic when it struck a deal with pharmaceutical company Pfizer to receive vaccines in exchange for health data.[6] As stated by the agreement, Israel allowed Pfizer to access its national health database to study "whether herd immunity is achieved after reaching a certain percentage of vaccination coverage in Israel". This provided the small country with accelerated access to vaccines while allowing the pharmaceutical company to compile large amounts of data about the safety and efficacy of its product.

Data Sharing vs. Data Privacy

No matter where you are in the world, the balance between sharing data and keeping it secure is difficult to address. Most countries have a legal framework for health data protection and public authorities are in charge granting access to national datasets. This can sometimes make it very challenging to use and share health data not only with private organizations but also across public authorities. For example, Israel explained in an OECD report that the committee in charge of evaluating data sharing projects often rejects them if they consider that patient privacy isn't protected enough.[7] Some countries need to create specific agreements each time data needs to be shared among public authorities while others exclude health data from all exchanges. When it comes to sharing data for research purposes, requirements can also vary from country to country. Most of them have specific approval processes that can be very lengthy and make it particularly challenging for foreign research organizations to access national datasets.

To address data privacy challenges, most countries rely on restrictive regulation. Two of the most well-known are the Health Insurance Portability and Accountability Act (HIPAA) in the US and the General Data Protection Regulation (GDPR) in the European Union. According to WHO research, 78% of countries worldwide have privacy protection policies for identifiable personal data, whether on paper or digital format.[8] However, the percentage drops to 54% when it comes to healthcare data. Therefore, despite the perception that health data is heavily regulated all over the world, research shows that it is not necessarily the case. The French data protection authority (CNIL) mapped data protection policies in various countries and concluded on their compatibility with the GDPR, which is considered as the most constraining personal data regulation worldwide (Figure 5.2). Switzerland, Argentina, and Japan are the only countries with perfectly adequate data protection systems when compared with the GDPR.[9]

Another key element in the data sharing vs. data privacy balance is the degree of control citizens have over their health data. This element has been investigated by the World Health Organization according to the following criteria in which individuals are:[10]

■ Provided electronic access to their own health-related data when held in an EHR;
■ Allowed to demand their own health-related data be corrected when held in an EHR if it is known to be inaccurate;
■ Allowed to demand the deletion of health-related data from their EHR; and
■ Allowed to specify which health-related data from their EHR can be shared with health professionals of their choice.

In most countries, health data has been treated as very sensitive and in the sole control of medical teams. However, this perception, as detailed in previous chapter, is slowly changing. Globally, only 29% of countries have legislation that allows individuals to access their own health data stored in EHRs. In addition, it is interesting to note that 28% of countries also answered that they have specific regulations that allow patients to decide which health providers can access their medical information. These countries are located mainly in Europe, the Americas, and Western Pacific. The World Health Organization notes that these same countries

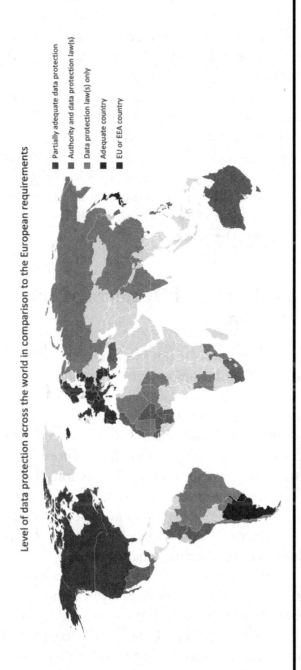

Figure 5.2 Level of GDPR compatibility in the world.

often stand for patient empowerment and patient-centred care, but they fail to translate it into practical measures. However, this percentage is expected to increase in the next couple of years are regulation evolves for more individual access and visibility over health data.

The list of challenges that various countries face when it comes to health data is endless: lack of standards, lack of resources, or technical capacities to conduct data analysis, poor data quality. However, despite these challenges, some countries succeeded in implementing ambitious digital health strategies with a strong focus on patients and their health data. In the next section we give three detailed examples: Estonia, France, and Denmark.

Creating a Fully Digital Democracy: The Example of Estonia

Researching the Estonian eHealth system online will lead you to catchy videos of all the online services an e-citizen has at its disposal. For instance, you can access the national health service online through your digital identity, connected to your unique personal identification code.[11] On your patient portal, you have access to your complete medical history and those of your relatives that have given you permission: doctor visits, imagery, lab exams, treatments, allergies, etc.[12] Health professionals and family/care-givers have access to this data unless you say otherwise and revoke permission. A truly patient-centred EHR data management system.

Among the other services offered by the Estonian health system, citizens can benefit from digital prescriptions that facilitate doctor-pharmacist communication and make refills easier but also from a digital ambulance service. Indeed, in case of an accident, the dispatcher can access a patient's medical records, with their unique ID and send the ambulance all the information they need to know about the victim. Access to this data can help the medical team make informed decisions and avoid errors. All this data is in turn poured into the patient's medical history so that doctors at the hospital can immediately know what happened and treat the patient accordingly.

The Estonian health services provide a seamless online experience. It looks like what most of us dream of when trying to imagine the ideal digital-driven health system: a single ID to access all services and portals, a unique repository for all medical data, accessibility to all approved health providers, portability abroad, and interoperability among all medical and paramedical professionals. But how does Estonia do it?

Estonia began its digital transformation over 20 years ago. In 1991, the country became independent from the Soviet Union and undertook a massive modernization process. With limited resources at its disposal, Estonia decided to build a cost-effective digital system from scratch. Without complex legacy systems to worry about, the country was able to deploy state-of-the-art services, starting by providing internet access to every school by 1998.

Estonia has universal health coverage for its citizens and spends approximately 6% of its GDP on health. Between 1991 and the beginning of the 21st century, health providers were encouraged to make use of the technology available to digitalize their practice and develop their own information systems. In parallel, the government started planning for a national digital health strategy and roadmap. From there, several successive and incremental milestones were set. Take the example of claims:[13]

- 2001: The Estonian Health Insurance Fund was set with an electronic claims management system;
- 2002: All pharmacies were required to electronically transfer their reimbursement claims to the EHIF; and

■ 2005: All claims across all health providers were required to be transferred electronically.

This system was developed over time, giving stakeholders the time to adapt to new processes and integrate innovation in their practice. This step-by-step approach could be one of the reasons why the digital health strategy became so successful and widely accepted in Estonia.

Investigating the structure of the Estonian system, we realized that it is based on three pillars that support and secure all digital services: digital ID, the X-Road, and the KSI blockchain.

Estonia is home to 1.3 million citizens and one of the most advanced digital societies in the world. Everything from voting, to registering a new car, to applying for a passport can be done online. Estonia's ambition is to develop the first fully digital public service. To do so, one of the main steps was to equip each citizen with a digital identity, linked to their physical ID card. But unlike in most countries where ID is only used as a proof of identification, in Estonia, it is the key to a myriad of online services and enables digital signatures which are recognized as equal to regular hand-written ones. Among the online services accessible through the online ID are taxes or health records. According to a CNBC report, this digital signature system has helped the government save 2% of GDP/year.[14]

The X-Road is a data exchange layer between multiple information systems. In Estonia, there is no central database gathering information produced by different public authorities. The reason is that creating a central repository also creates a single point of failure that can take the system down if it is attacked. Instead, data remains where it is created, and different databases are connected between them through the X-Road. Initially, this choice was driven by economic and governance considerations. Creating a central and powerful middleware system appeared more expensive than building a decentralized and smaller solution. In addition, a centralized system required a custodian to manage operations. Since no governmental agency could endorse this role alone, it was decided that it would be a shared governance system in which all players are involved. But the benefits are now clear: the X-Road allows all public authorities to use data that lies outside of their system to provide seamless services in record time. For instance, the population register might need information from the health service or vice-versa. Through the X-Road, although the information is not stored and managed together, it is still accessible when needed. This system relied on a few prerequisites. First, data must only be accessible to the parties that need to access it. Second, it must not be modified while shared to ensure data integrity in time. Third, data must be protected from third parties while in transit with adequate privacy and security measures. In other words, governmental agencies need to be able to communicate with one another without worrying about their exchanges being exposed. From a technical perspective, the X-Road makes interoperability easier. Indeed, as explained by Andres Kütt, one of the architects of Estonia's information system, in an educational video, when two different organizations use different standards to record information, it becomes nearly impossible for them to communicate with one another.[15] X-Road solves this problem by acting like a translator between the two. According to the e-Estonia Briefing Centre, the X-Road saves Estonians 844 years of working time every year.[16] In addition, this technology is now also used in Finland, Iceland, and Japan.

In Estonia, the X-Road is complemented by a blockchain that secures information and ensures that no data is manipulated. It was first developed in 2008, way before anyone had heard about cryptocurrencies or bitcoin, and it is one of the key components of public trust in governmental entities. Indeed, blockchain is known for creating tamper-proof ledgers of information that no one can alter. By creating this immutable and transparent base for all exchanges and transactions with public authorities, the Estonian government developed a trustworthy relationship with its citizens. This blockchain backbone is particularly useful in building a patient-centred health system in which patients have more control and visibility over their data.

These three pillars make Estonia a truly data-driven State with effective and efficient administrations as well as trust from the general public. Access, exchange, and use of data is facilitated in a secure environment. In a recent discussion with a fellow digital health expert, we were even told that in Estonia, you will never be asked for the same information twice. That made me smile, thinking of the million times we had to provide our addresses, dates of birth, or social security numbers to the public authorities in our home country! But besides it being handy for citizens, it also implies that governmental agencies do not have to collect the same information repeatedly. Transpose this to the health systems, and it means that hospitals do not have to run the same tests each time you step foot into a new facility or see a new doctor. When considering the astronomic costs associated with this flaw in the system, the resultant saving could be equally impressive.

The core of the Estonian digital health system is the online medical record accessible to patients through a dedicated portal. Through the use of multiple technological bricks, among which blockchain, each patient can set access rights to their medical records. To facilitate this access control management, a patient's health professionals have access to their medical records by default. Should a patient want to revoke access, they can simply do it through the portal. This system allows patients that want more control to exercise it while removing the burden of data management from those that accept the system as it is. In addition, patients are also asked if they agree to share their anonymized data for research purposes. However, this feature is quite limited as it only offers a yes/no option. Consequently, patients who wish to dispose of more precise control abilities will tend to refuse data sharing. The Estonian authorities are now looking into ways to implement dynamic consent that will provide patients with the capacity to better control the conditions in which their data is shared.

Although Estonia looks like an incredible digital health success story, the country did face some challenges when it first implemented this strategy.[17] For example, to increase data interoperability, health providers had to change the way they fill in their medical records. They were required to use a more unified language and make sure to follow best practices. This process took some time and faced resistance from some members of the medical community. Moreover, just like in other countries, not all health providers were familiar with digital solutions, and it required time and effort to increase digital health literacy.

One of the key success factors of the Estonian model is the trust citizens place in their e-government. As thoroughly discussed in this book, it is the core of any digital and data-driven health system accepted by patients. In a survey conducted in 2020, 82% of citizens said they trust the digital services provided by the Estonian government.[18] However, it is interesting to note that trust in the government itself is at only 43%, close to the OECD average. These figures show that although citizens can disagree with the country's politics, they do trust the underlying technological infrastructures and the services they leverage. According to Estonian officials, this trust was built step by step, deploying services one after the other and taking the time to communicate about them and educate on their use.[19] They also added that the government uses non-formal means of communication such as emails to create proximity and interaction with their fellow citizens. In addition, transparency and security are key. Estonia relies on high levels of cybersecurity measures, timestamping, and traceability and transparency of their databases. However, Estonia knows that public trust is a fragile asset and continues to improve its processes to maintain it over time.

How France Redesigned Its Digital Health Roadmap from the Ground Up

The patient's role within the health system has largely evolved in France since the middle of the 20th century. Up until then, patients were merely the recipients of care, and their preferences, doubts, and choices were rarely considered, as clearly stated by the President of the French College of Physicians in 1950: "The user is notoriously incapable. It belongs to the doctor to decide what is good for him".[20] Thankfully, the situation has evolved ever since, and citizens, as both beneficiaries and contributors to the national public health services, are increasingly involved in governance and decision-making. Moreover, France is considered to have one of the largest health databases in the world, with medico-administrative information from over 65 million citizens.[21]

After the Second World War, the French health system began undergoing a profound transformation towards a more patient-centred model. The goal was to turn hospitals into pivots of the health system and patients into the subject of care rather than its object. This movement was accelerated in the '80s at the dawn of many health crises taken up by the media (AIDS, Creutzfeldt–Jakob disease, etc.).[22] Patients' movements started taking more and more place, and for the first time the balance of power was reversed between citizens and medical experts. These events lead to a critical moment in the French patients' history: March 4th, 2002, a law, also called Kouchner law, redesigned the health system and set the basis of the French health democracy. It strengthened the patient's rights to information and consent and allowed increased user's participation in public health policies. Ever since, additional laws supported citizen involvement in the health system. In parallel, patients' associations emerged and reinforced the user's voice in decision-making processes regarding the healthcare system. They were given a seat at the table in major public health institutions and contributed to defining new policies, promoting biomedical research respectful of patient's rights, or developing citizen-centred initiatives.

In 2004, France made its first important move towards the digitalization of its health system by creating the Dossier Médical Personnel (DMP) the national electronic health record.[23] Its goal was to gather a patient's medical information and make it accessible across all health professionals and organizations. Behind this goal lies the willingness to reduce unnecessary duplication of medical exams, avoid medical errors associated with a lack of information about a patient and ultimately reduce costs. However, the DMP encountered difficult beginnings fuelled by concerns about the perimeter of information it should contain, the importance given to data protection, its accessibility by different stakeholders or its technical feasibility.[24] In 2007, an audit provided with severe conclusions and highlighted the need to rebuild the DMP on more solid grounds. As a result, in 2008 a new working team was created focused on developing a data sharing tool between health professionals with little role given to patients. Despite these new efforts, the DMP fails to meet its adoption objectives and the project is placed on hold in 2012. In 2017, the DMP, renamed Dossier Médical Partagé, is given yet another shot at success and the national health insurance is made responsible for its deployment. This new approach has been more successful than the previous ones: as of April 2019, 5 million French citizens opened their DMP.

The French digital health strategy benefited from a new boost in 2018, as President Emmanuel Macron announced the "Ma Santé 2022" plan, a reform of the health system with a strong focus on its digitalization.[25] The roadmap included key measures such as redefining the governance of digital health with a focus on involving all stakeholders, intensifying the security and the interoperability of information systems, accelerating the deployment of digital health platforms and key services such as the DMP and stimulating innovation and engagement.[26] From this roadmap have ensued several actions that are still in progress today. For instance, fundamental technological bricks are developed to create unique IDs for patients and health professionals across all facilities, ensure interoperability of privately and publicly developed solutions and guarantee the security of data flows. On top of that, a cluster of services are deployed, including the DMP, e-prescription or secured messaging.[27] These services will support the out roll of three major platforms dedicated to citizens, health professionals, and health data organizations. The Espace Numérique de Santé, is the patient-facing component that provides them with public and private health services (DMP, telehealth, agenda, disease management apps, etc.), management of their health data, and more engagement in the care pathway.

Another key component of this new vision is the health data platform called Health Data Hub. The Health Data Hub was created in 2019 with the goal of facilitating access to a multitude of disparate and heterogenous data sources scattered across the health system[28]. Prior to its creation, France had one of the most important health databases in the world called the Health Data National System (SNDS). It gathered data from the health insurance (SNIIRAM database); hospitals (PMSI database); medical causes of death (database of Inserm's CépiDC) and data relating to disability (data from the CNSA)[29]. However, these databases, initially developed for

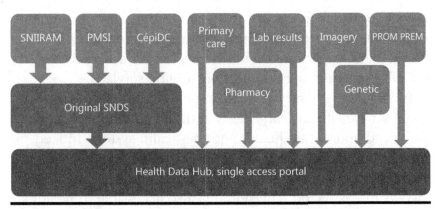

Figure 5.3 Datasets in the French Health Data Hub.

administrative purposes, contained no clinical data and didn't reflect the variety of information that can now be accessible about the population. This created a major obstacle to innovation, especially in the field of artificial intelligence. As a result, public authorities created the Health Data Hub designed to gather and linkage various sources of data, including the SNDS, to accelerate research and innovation. Designed as the unique counter for all health data related initiatives, the Hub matches data users with data producers and provides the ecosystem with complementary services. With time, it is destined to contain much more than data from the historic SNDS (Figure 5.3).

This new roadmap places the State as the provider of fundamental technological features, services, and platforms on which all other stakeholders can build on. If France succeeds in turning this vision into a reality, it could become one of the most advanced and operational digital health systems in the world.

The Data-Driven Danish System

Denmark is considered to have one of the most digitally advanced health systems in the world. The Scandinavian country provides free access to healthcare to all its 5.8 million inhabitants. At birth, all Danish citizens are provided with a unique national ID, but they can also ask for a web-ID that will allow them to access all public online services.

In 2003, the country launched sundhed.dk, an eHealth portal where citizens can access and find all the information they need about their health and the health system. Indeed, among the functionalities of this portal, citizens can access their medical history but also benefit from different services such as telemedicine. The portal is also accessible to health professionals that can gain controlled access to the medical data of their patients.[30] One of Sundhed.dk's main ambitions is to aggregate a large volume of data and facilitate access to it.[31] For example, the patient-facing interface gathers various data sources such as lab exams, imagery, or prescription data. This system relies on a solid infrastructure that was pre-existing and included data communication standards and qualitative datasets.

One of the success factors of Sundhed.dk is that it engaged multiple stakeholders, representative of the Danish health system. Initially, all regions worked together to set a common ambition and reach a uniform level of digitalization. Sundhed. dk faced some challenges because of the different local projects that were already developed but weren't compatible with the new platform. With time, hundreds of different partners joined Sundhed.dk, giving the portal a strong legitimacy and footprint in the national eHealth environment. Nevertheless, this also created challenges as some parties had divergent interests that Sundhed.dk has to manage and align.

According to OECD research, Denmark is the country with the highest rate of health data availability, maturity, and use.[32] The national health database includes comprehensive information such as in-patient records, prescriptions, disease registries, etc. Patient-reported outcomes (PROs) are collected either by sending patients an online survey or providing them with a tablet in hospital waiting rooms. In some regions, PROs are even included in the EHR, and Denmark considers the collection and integration of PROs to current systems as a priority. The country is creating a national bank for all PRO surveys that physicians and researchers can use. Nearly all clinical terminology is coded and included almost in real-time in the national database, allowing public authorities to efficiently monitor the quality of care and the performance of the health system at a national level. Moreover, Denmark is one of the rare countries that regularly link their datasets for monitoring and research purposes.

In 2018, the Danish government launched a new national strategy for digital health focused on the use of health data for better prevention and care[33]. One of the key enablers of this digital strategy is active patient engagement. Sundhed.dk will play a critical role, by continuing to connect different data sources both from hospitals and private practices to provide patients with a full overview of their health pathway. Denmark also developed other digital health services adapted to the patient's needs and expectations. For example, the "doctor in your pocket" app connects citizens to different GPs for online consultations. The app was designed as a simple interface for the doctor–patient relation. Not only does it provide telemedicine services with it can also be used for prescriptions and secure messaging. Another key focus of the digital health strategy is data privacy and security. Today, Danish citizens do not have visibility over which health professional accessed their medical records at the hospital. This is something that will soon change. Indeed, the digital health strategy states that the log information needs to be displayed on a patient portal, such as Sundhed.dk so that citizens can see which member of the medical staff saw their health data. The goal is not only to improve data security, but also to discourage unjustified access to medical records. In addition to that, authorities also included in their roadmap the development of tools that give patients better control over their health data.

After looking into these countries, we asked ourselves a question: what is for us one essential ingredient for a successful digital health strategy? Our answer: to envision digital health outside of the technological and regulatory considerations. The countries that have created and implemented successful digital health strategies, had a holistic approach that included education, communication, governance, cultural factors, etc. Often, countries are so focused on building the technological bricks and fitting into the legal framework that they forget that success is highly dependent on citizen's acceptance. The focus should therefore also be placed on educating health providers and empowering patients in the digital world. As seen with the Estonian model, citizens need to be part of the digital transformation journey. They need to be educated on the individual and collective advantages of digital health, they need to be made aware of the new services available and they need to feel reassured that the government operates in a trustworthy and transparent way. Of course, this is not a miracle solution, or a one size fits all model. Each country is at a different starting point with different strategies, different cultural approaches, and different challenges. Undeniably, in order to move past these barriers, strong political will, and leadership, coupled with appropriate resources, whether human or financial, are necessary to transform strategies into reality.

Notes

1 OECD. 2019. Health in the 21st century: putting data to work for stronger health systems, OECD Health Policy Studies, OECD Publishing, Paris. doi:10.1787/e3b23f8e-en
2 Oderkirk J. 2021. Survey results: national health data infrastructure and governance, OECD Health Working Papers, No. 127, OECD Publishing, Paris. doi:10.1787/55d24b5d-en

3 Peterson A MSc, et al. Collaboratively improving diabetes care in Sweden using a national quality register. *Qual Manag Health Care*. 2015;24(4):212–221.

4 Svensson AM. The Swedish national diabetes register: 20 years of successful improvements, https://www.ndr.nu/pdfs/20%20 years%20of%20successful%20improvements_lowres_singelpage. pdf (accessed October 2021).

5 Comstock J. A 'gold mine' of data is driving Israel's billion-shekel bet on digital health, *MobiHealthNews*, https://www. mobihealthnews.com/news/emea/gold-mine-data-driving-israels-billion-shekel-bet-digital-health (accessed November 2021).

6 Real-world epidemiological evidence collaboration agreement between the State of Israel and Pfizer, https://govextra.gov.il/ media/30806/11221-moh-pfizer-collaboration-agreement-redacted.pdf (accessed November 2021).

7 Oderkirk J. 2021. Survey results: national health data infrastructure and governance, OECD Health Working Papers, No. 127, OECD Publishing, Paris. doi:10.1787/55d24b5d-en

8 World Health Organization. Global diffusion of eHealth: making universal health coverage achievable: report of the third global survey on eHealth, https://apps.who.int/iris/ handle/10665/252529?search-result=true&query=global+survey+ ehealth&scope=%2F&rpp=10&sort_by=score&order=desc (accessed October 2021).

9 CNIL, La protection des données dans le monde, https://www. cnil.fr/fr/la-protection-des-donnees-dans-le-monde (accessed October 2021).

10 World Health Organization. Global diffusion of eHealth: making universal health coverage achievable: report of the third global survey on eHealth, https://apps.who.int/iris/ handle/10665/252529?search-result=true&query=global+survey+ ehealth&scope=%2F&rpp=10&sort_by=score&order=desc (accessed October 2021).

11 E-estonia website, Healthcare, eHealth Record, https:// e-estonia.com/solutions/healthcare/e-health-records/ (accessed October 2021).

12 E-estonia YouTube channel, An Overview of eHealth Services in Estonia https://www.youtube.com/watch?v=H4QLzQGMI3k (accessed October 2021).

13 Metsallik J, Ross P, Draheim D, Piho G. Ten Years of the eHealth System in Estonia, http://ceur-ws.org/Vol-2336/MMHS2018_invited.pdf (accessed October 2021).

14 Schulze E. How a tiny country bordering Russia became one of the most tech-savvy societies in the world, *CNBC*, https://www.cnbc.com/2019/02/08/how-estonia-became-a-digital-society.html (accessed October 2021).

15 TalTech õppematerjalid / study materials YouTube channel, X-road architecture (technological approach) by Andres Kütt, https://www.youtube.com/watch?v=WDk4Ik41IDs (accessed October 2021).

16 E-estonia website, Digitalisation isn't instagrammable – and that's a problem, https://e-estonia.com/speakers-corner-digitalisation-isnt-instagrammable/ (accessed November 2021).

17 Metsallik J, Ross P, Draheim D, Piho G. Ten Years of the eHealth System in Estonia, http://ceur-ws.org/Vol-2336/MMHS2018_invited.pdf (accessed October 2021).

18 E-estonia website, How do you build trust in government? https://e-estonia.com/building-trust-in-government/ (accessed November 2021).

19 E-estonia website, The cornerstone of e-governance is trust, https://e-estonia.com/cornerstone-governance-trust/ (accessed November 2021).

20 Place de l'usager dans le système de santé, https://www.gipse.eu/documents/wa_files/3%20la%20place%20de%20lusager%20dans%20le%20systeme%20de%20sante.pdf (accessed November 2021).

21 Moulis G, Lapeyre-Mestre M, Palmaro A, Pugnet G, Montastruc J-L, Sailler L. French health insurance databases: what interest for medical research? *La Revue de Médecine Interne.* 2015;36(6):411–417. ISSN 0248-8663. doi:10.1016/j.revmed.2014.11.009

22 Ministère des Solidarités et de la Santé, L'historique depuis 1945, https://solidarites-sante.gouv.fr/systeme-de-sante-et-medico-social/parcours-de-sante-vos-droits/les-usagers-et-leurs-representants/article/l-historique-depuis-1945 (Accessed October 2021).

23 Vie publique, Dossier médical partagé: une mise en oeuvre sur deux décennies, https://www.vie-publique.fr/eclairage/18471-dossier-medical-partage-dmp-une-mise-en-oeuvre-sur-deux-decennies (accessed October 2021).

24 Cacot P. Les enseignements d'une histoire récente: l'utopie du DMP. *Les Tribunes de la santé.* 2016;51:89–98. doi:10.3917/seve.051.0089

25 Ministère des Solidartiés et de la Santé, Ma santé 2022: un engagement collectif, https://solidarites-sante.gouv.fr/systeme-de-sante-et-medico-social/masante2022/ (accessed October 2021).

26 Ministère des Solidarités et de la Santé, Dossier d'information feuille de route "Accélérer le virage numérique", https://solidarites-sante.gouv.fr/IMG/pdf/190425_dossier_presse_masante2022_ok.pdf (accessed October 2021).

27 FEHAP, Le Sénat fait du DMP une composante incontournable de l'ENS, https://www.fehap.fr/jcms/activites-services/etablisse-ments-services/systemes-d-information-de-sante/services-nationaux-socles/dmp/le-senat-fait-du-dmp-un-composant-a-part-entiere-de-l-ens-fehap_310099 (accessed October 2021).

28 CNIL, La Plateforme des données de santé (Health Data Hub), https://www.cnil.fr/fr/la-plateforme-des-donnees-de-sante-health-data-hub (accessed October 2021).

29 Health Data Hub. Qu'est-ce que le SNDS? https://www.health-data-hub.fr/snds (accessed October 2021).

30 Sundhed.dk, Background, https://www.sundhed.dk/borger/service/om-sundheddk/om-organisationen/ehealth-in-denmark/background/ (accessed October 2021).

31 Jensen TB, Thorseng AA. Building national healthcare infra-structure: the case of the Danish eHealth portal. 2017 May 12. In: Aanestad M, Grisot M, Hanseth O, et al. editors. *Information Infrastructures within European Health Care: Working with the Installed Base [Internet].* Cham (CH): Springer; 2017. Chapter 13. Available from: https://www.ncbi.nlm.nih.gov/books/NBK543679/. doi: 10.1007/978-3-319-51020-0_13

32 Oderkirk J. 2021. Survey results: national health data infrastruc-ture and governance, OECD Health Working Papers, No. 127, OECD Publishing, Paris. doi:10.1787/55d24b5d-en

33 Healthcare Denmark, Danish Digital Health Strategy 2018-2022 now available in English, https://www.healthcaredenmark.dk/news/danish-digital-health-strategy-2018-2022-now-available-in-english/ (accessed November 2021).

Afterword

Our book, focused on patient empowerment through digital health, cannot rule out that the one key piece of patient empowerment is access to healthcare, a fundamental human right. The reality is that access to care varies by country, region, wealth of the nation, personal wealth, race, and other factors. It is convoluted, let alone political. We debated whether we should dedicate a chapter to this but realized that we would not be able to do it justice. Access to care is a big topic that many experts have written about in books, assays, etc. and it is also a whole curriculum taught in the universities. Therefore, we decided to focus the book on digital health but only brushed on the surface the challenges of accessing care that some people might take for granted.

Over the past ten years, the world has seen an increase of digital solutions and with the pandemic it has created an opportunity to accelerate digital innovation and the use of telehealth, devices, wearables, sensors, artificial intelligence to diagnose diseases, etc. Mobile Health, or "mHealth", has rocketed, and it is forecasted to be worth US$100 billion in the next few years. This is just the start of the patient health revolution and the evolution of the future of healthcare and its ecosystem.

DOI:10.4324/9781003215868-6

There has been a lot of hype on patient empowerment and digital health with many new start-ups surfacing and providing a sort of niche services or solutions. It is almost as if new technologies have unleashed the power of health data when it was always right in front of us. The only difference is that now we have new and better technologies that are able to handle large quantities of data, use of open APIs, adoption of frameworks to use common standards, etc.

We know that aggregating and sharing data can improve diagnoses, lead to new discoveries, and strengthen scientific results including in clinical trials for rare diseases. The World Health Organization has stressed the importance of ensuring data interoperability. However, the complex and dynamic regulatory landscape of data privacy and local laws tends to complicate data collection, sharing, and utilization. Technologies like federated data systems, and the development of common technical and regulatory standards, could help address this problem. But this is just one of the big issues. As described in Chapter 5, there is still a lot we need to do to accomplish this. Leaders (government) in the digital health space are acknowledging the much-needed interoperability and data sharing from local to national and national to transnational. There are good initiatives that started the discussion, but the reality is that this will take years to change the national guidance, systems, and processes before we even look at cross-nation. It is almost as painful as the UN global climate summits, COPs (Conference of the Parties). You know the benefits and it must be done but how do you get everyone onboard, committed, and ensure the long-term investment?

According to the World Economic Forum, the evolution of healthcare will depend on the sustainability of healthcare systems, preserving health, enabling access to health, preparing for, and responding to epidemic, and healthcare technologies. When we talk about sustainability of healthcare systems, we need to think how governments and society can continue to maintain the equilibrium to preserve health. In an ideal world, we empower patients to manage their health and work in collaboration with their medical team or healthcare practitioners, institutions, health providers, insurance/payers, and overall collaborating with the different stakeholders in their 'health ecosystem'. Patients taking control of their health with information shared with them, working closely as partners, and not as a subject. The reality is that not many people will be onboard to taking that control, some might still prefer that their doctors make decisions for them. Others might take the extreme view of wanting to manage all their data and consenting to every request to grant access to their information, this makes the process inefficient and let alone the complexity to design systems like that. Who has the money and time? There will always be disparate opinions and especially on the ownership of data. On this latter topic, through the interviews and various discussions, there are different opinions. On health data (pseudo-anonymized or not), some believe that they own their data as they paid for services. Others think that any doctor's notes, etc. are about them, not from them; therefore, they don't own it. If we place the ownership on the person that generates the information, it is like saying, "I have oil in my land but the person that refines the oil will ultimately own it". We would not agree with that concept. If we start with pseudo-anonymized data, some have the view that this type of data should be shared freely, no consent would be needed from patients. Also, some say that when patients are consenting to share their data, pseudo-anonymized should be treated differently where patients would need to opt-out rather than opt-in, very un-GDPR. The process gets more complicated when the data is shared from data controllers to data consumers/users. Data governance around patient data becomes so critical in every country, it is literally a matter of life and death. The way governments dictate who owns patient data, what, and how it can be shared, could impact research, improving quality of care, diagnosis, better treatment, etc. So, before supporting one way or the other, remember, we are all patients at one stage in our lives, what would benefit you, your family's health, your friends' health, etc?

We often get asked how much patients should be paid for their data. In the book, we talk about patients wanting to be compensated but we never quantified the value. Also, compensation does not necessarily mean monetary. There is also the concern from researchers and organizations that if patients are being paid, it might lend itself to abuse especially for the vulnerable population. If we explore the path of patients to be compensated, quantifying it would not be an easy thing to do especially for real-world data. What is the fair market value? What or how will the data be used for? Should there be a time limit on access or usage of the data? In contrast, clinical trials, there is a more direct benefit for patients that participate. Time and travel expenses are paid for, full health checks, and medical teams available to them during the conduct of clinical trials. Their data collected would be used to bring a new drug or therapy into the market. Talking to patients and some patient advocacy groups, many patients are willing to share their data for free to advance research if the intent of use is clear and the benefits are shared.

There is a need to change healthcare policies related to data collection, sharing, and usage. There needs to be a broader campaign on health literacy and digital literacy. Also to include patient engagement and education on what and how data is collected, shared, used, and re-used or repurposed. Providing transparency will build trust that could further inform patients, but also decrease healthcare costs from early diagnosis to right treatment (personalized medicine), gene therapy and others.

A Look into 2050

In a future world where health has a whole new meaning, not only about prevention and maintaining health but also personalizing your needs to enhance your health, collecting your medical information seamlessly and providing real-time information to you and reporting it directly to your medical team. This is using technologies that can be easily interoperable that can be used to continuously monitor your health such as sensors placed in all the rooms of your home to monitor vital signs such as breath rate, heart rate, temperature, blood pressure, mood levels, and make the right recommendations that suit each person; also removing the need to go to the hospital for a scan or x-ray, and instead do it at your own home using a self-scan that can detect any abnormalities; and further, use devices that collect micro-samples of blood, saliva, etc. to assess your levels of cholesterol, liver function, all the biochemistry and haematology assessments. Use of technologies like AI to aggregate all that data and easily share the information with you and report to your medical or health team. AI can go beyond recommending treatment, diets, and wellness in general. In other words, your health team is no longer your traditional doctors, nurses, pathologist, pharmacists, in other words humans with medical background, but now includes AI, technology companies and device companies that build medical devices that include AI that will support your health and your quality of life. It is a hybrid medical team with more precise information about you, real-time assessment, and decision-making for your health and wellness.

It is like a sci-fi movie, but it is becoming more a reality with the current technologies and research, we are heading towards this trajectory. Are we far from that realization? The last two years we have seen a boom in technology at an unprecedented pace. With support from medical experts, technical experts, and researchers we have advanced health innovation, but we are still at the beginning of this exciting journey.

Gene editing is another big breakthrough. With over 10,000 diseases that have been identified, including some rare, we are curing less than 1%. Imagining a world where we have access to health data including genomics data, and through the power of data we are able to find cures for chronic diseases, cancer, and rare diseases, we would not only be saving lives and reducing the cost of care but transforming the healthcare system.

Think big and never settle for less. Demand for better care and treatment, access of information, be involved, and help others to become more educated about their health.

To our readers, we would like to thank you for your time dedicated to reading our book. Our intention is to create awareness and remove barriers to have engaging discussions for a better health ecosystem. We hope that we managed to achieve that.

Index

Page numbers in italics refer figures, Page numbers in **bold** refer tables.

Printed in the United States
by Baker & Taylor Publisher Services